A Stroke and I

JOANNA BARNES

Order this book online at www.trafford.com
or email orders@trafford.com

Most Trafford titles are also available at major online book retailers.

Printed in the United States of America.

ISBN: 978-1-4669-7357-2 (sc)
ISBN: 978-1-4669-7356-5 (e)

Trafford rev. 12/29/2012

 www.trafford.com

North America & international
toll-free: 1 888 232 4444 (USA & Canada)
phone: 250 383 6864 ♦ fax: 812 355 4082

Contents

A New Start

I lived in a town in the county of Surrey called Addlestone. This is getting bigger every year because of the building of houses and the growth of the population of people, but everything has to change doesn't it? Anyway, I lived in a maisonette called 'Hampshire Court'. There were two other maisonettes like the one I lived in and they were called 'Middlesex Court' and 'Sussex Court'. To make us all at home there was a tower block in the middle of Hampshire Court and Middlesex Court and this was called 'Surrey Towers'. There are sixteen floors to this block of flats, but the lifts only go up to the fifteenth floor and then you have to get out of the lifts and walk up to the sixteenth floor. It is a bit of a pain especially if you have a load of shopping. This was the only tower block in Addlestone (when I lived there) and from the top you could see for miles around, and further up the road is a place called Essex Close. We don't have anything to do with the people that live in this 'Close', I don't know why I think it is because they called us named so we called them names (silly names), so they kept themselves to themselves and we kept ourselves to ourselves. Anyway back to my home in Hampshire Court, I lived in the third one in from the road (number 15), inside I had my own bedroom (the smallest one out of the three) because I was the only girl in the family, but I didn't mind. My two brothers shared the middle sized bedroom and my mum and dad had the biggest bedroom (which was obvious because the parents always get the largest room).

Before I start my story of my life let me tell you about myself and my family. First of all let me tell you about myself, I am an only girl in a family of five: two brothers, a mother and a father. I am the smallest member of my family, but that doesn't bother me because they say that all good things come in small parcels. Anyway back to my family. My mum, her name was Jacquelyn (Jackie for short) she was 5foot 3 inches tall and was a very large woman with dark hair that was going grey very quickly but she was always dying it different colours to hide the grey hairs. When I get to the stage of going grey I will go grey naturally and not bother hiding it because I think that going grey is part of growing older and that is part of life. Anyway the job that she used to do was a lolly-pop lady (crossing-person) that was until she got too old to do it anymore. Now my dad, his name was Keith, he was 5foot 5 inches tall and was a very fit man, mind you he had to be a fit man to do the job that he did; you see he was a milkman from the year 1973 until 2010. Now for my two brothers, Stephen and Kevin; Kevin was always the naughty one out of the three of us so he was the one that was getting into trouble. Kevin when he was younger looked like a sweet child because he had little curls in his brown hair, whereas Stephen was just like a normal boy with his normal brown hair; he was the oldest out of the three of us.

That is enough about my family now for my life story . . . .

1972

It was late hours of the 17th of January evening night when my mother went into labour with guess who, you've guessed it ME. I didn't finally decide to come out until the 18th the same birthdate as my Grandfather Hoy (my mum's dad). Fancy that me having the same birthday as one of my grandparents, what a privilege it will be for me to share such a special day, I feel such a lucky girl. Of course I didn't know it at the time because I had just been born, but I will look forward to it in years to come.

For the next three years I do not remember much except for 1974 when my mum gave birth to my younger brother, Kevin Dennis Norgate. I do know I made special friends with a girl who lived two doors way from where I lived, her name was Sandra. She was born 29 days after I was, on the 16th February 1972, but she was much bigger than I was but I never minded because she became my best friend.

1974

This year was quite an exciting year because my mum was pregnant with my younger brother, Kevin Dennis Norgate. My dad had just recently started a new job at being a milkman. It was in the middle of the year when Kevin was born. In fact it was on the same date as our Nan Norgate's birthday the 20th June. So that meant Kevin had to share his birthday and so did I, but I did not mind. I don't know whether Kevin did or not?

1975-6

The first thing I can remember is when I was at nursery school in Addlestone; I was playing with my best friend Sandra. Sandra was a sweet girl (like me), with blonde hair (like me, at the time). We could have been have been have mistaken for twins, that's how alike we were, but things change. The nursery school was an old church that was converted in to a nursery school. It had girls/boys toilets, a cloak room to hang our coats in. It even had a headmaster/mistress room where all the records were kept. Anyway, Sandra and I were best friends and this particular time we were in the sand pit, when suddenly I picked up some sand and throw it at Sandra's face. I don't know why I did this but this made Sandra cry, so I saw Sandra crying and this made me cry even though it was my fault Sandra was crying in the first place. You see Sandra and I were like sisters because we have known each other since birth and whenever the other one was away due to illness or something the other one used to get upset. It was like that all the way through the primary school, we used to miss each other like anything if the other one was away, even if they were in another class.

The next memory I got was when we were at nursery and we used to get the third pints of milk that was until Margaret Thatcher of the Conservative Party stopped us from getting it. Anyway, there was one of the milks that had gone off and I was last in the queue to get the milk and I got the milk that had gone off. It made me sick and I didn't finish the milk because it was bad all the way through. Luckily everyone else had finished their milk and had gone to do the activity they were doing before, so only the monitor and me had noticed me being sick.

Another memory I have for this year was my birthday, I remember this day because I shared it with another girl called Rebecca. I remember this girl because well I wouldn't say she was slow but she was not top of the class, well I wouldn't say that I was top of the class but I was not as bottom as she was. We both celebrated our birthday with a birthday cake; mine was bigger than hers was because hers was shop brought and mine was home made because my mum made mine. Thank you mum for making my cake, it was beautiful in taste and in sight. Thank you.

1977-8

I had grown up a year when I had another memory. It was in the first year of our Darley Dene Primary School, Addlestone, Surrey. We were in a proper classroom now, with desks and chairs, whereas in the nursery school we mainly had cushions and toys to play around on. Anyway, my best friend Sandra and I had finished our work, so we were told to sit on the mat and read a book. So Sandra and I sat on the mat but instead of reading a book we decided to play 'oranges and lemons'. This is a game that all little children learnt how to play when they were in nursery school. We got told off badly and told to stand in the corner, well we both did this but Sandra was crying and me well I stood in the corner picking my nose and sticking it on the wall. Well I was only about six at the time. When it came to classes for the following year they split Sandra and I up, I don't know why, perhaps it was because of all the fun we got up to, who knows?

1978-9

I can remember going to school in the January of 1979 when we had some snow from the December 1978. My mum and younger brother had come over to my classroom because the nursery that Kevin went too had been cancelled due to the snow. Stephen had walked to his school (Sayes Court Middle School, Addlestone), so whether or not his school is open or close my mum has to find out. Anyway back to my school, I had got into my classroom and found the milk (back in those days we were allowed a little bottle of milk), so I found the straws and put them into the milk. I wasn't to know that there was no school for the rest of the week, so it was a waste of time me doing the milk.

One thing I used to really enjoy was the music lesson. I used to look forward to this because the whole class used to join in and sing along with the recording. I can remember this one particular day I was sitting next to this boy called Peter Fielder and he kept the pamphlet to himself he would not let me read the words to the songs. So I tried to pull the pamphlet and where he held it tight he ripped it. I told the teacher and he got a good telling off and told to pay for a new set of pamphlets; it was not my fault that the pamphlet got ripped. This happened in the second year.

1979-80

When it came to the third year of the Darley Dene Primary School my mum came with me one morning to see my teacher about something, I now know what it was. I remember this day because it was just after my birthday in January. It was to tell my teacher that my grandfather Hoy had died and that I might be a bit upset because he was my favourite grandfather. What I don't know was how I am supposed to be a bit upset about my grandfather if I don't even know he is even dead when no one has told me. I was not even allowed to go to his funeral that is what upset me the most.

One thing I can remember about my brother, Stephen and saying naughty words, well they were classed as naughty words when we were younger. Well on this particular day we were playing out the back of our maisonette when Stephen said that I 'farted' when I didn't, and he carried on saying it. Now I got upset over this that I ran in doors crying. My mum and dad asked what the matter was so I told them what Stephen did. So my dad called Stephen in and asked him what he had said, so he told him. You know the saying that they will wash your mouth out with soap and water; well my dad washed Stephen's mouth out with washing-up liquid. Stephen never said things like that again.

1980-1

Another thing I remember from the third year in Darley Dene Primary School is when it came to the a lesson where the girls did needle work and the boys well I can't remember what they did but I know they did something that they girls didn't do. Anyway, the girls made all sorts of thing in needle work such as: an apron, a doll, a pencil case etc.

One thing I do remember enjoying about Darley Dene School is the Christmas plays because Sandra and I used to do our bit by playing in the orchestra by playing the recorder. I don't know how I managed to play it because I just copied Sandra most of the time but the music teacher must have thought I was some good otherwise she would not have put me in the orchestra. I can remember one of the plays: Jack and the beanstalk. It was really good because the teacher who did the play got the tallest boy in the third year to be the giant, and it was quite funny at times.

When I was in my Darley Dene Primary School one thing I hated about break times and lunch times was the time we had to play around. The reason why I hated these times was because of two girls, Debbie and Katie, they always picking on me; I don't know why but they always were ganging up on me. Sandra used to go around with them too, but on the sly she came up to me and told me that she was still my friend, and I believed her.

There was one thing that I remember from my primary school that affected the whole of my family. Well I say the whole of my family, it only really affected my mum and dad, and that was a car crash. My dad went to pick my mum up and was on their way home, when a car went past them at high speed and knocked them off the road. Their car went rolling down the hill with them inside it. They got off with cuts and bruises, my dad had a few broken ribs, but apart from that they got of lightly. The police got the driver of the other car; he got sentenced with dangerous driving and carrying an offensive weapon, because he was carrying a knife in his car.

Out the back of our maisonette there were some sheds for the people, who lived upstairs, but most of them were empty and the doors of them were broken or vandalised, so we used to play around in them, making up games such as families, or a game I used to like playing called 'ghost'. This game one person used to be a normal person going around the building and the other people have to go round and frighten that person by pretending to be a ghost. Now there was this one time I was a 'ghost' and my brother Stephen was the normal person. I was hiding around this corner and Stephen didn't see me, he went to walk straight past me and I jumped out at him and frightened the living daylights out of him. I haven't frightened anyone as much as I had frightened him before in my life. I know it was a wicked thing to do but I found it very funny even now when I think about it.

While all this was happening my two brothers and I were still at school. My younger brother and I were at Darley Dene Primary School, while my elder brother was at Sayes Court Middle School. A friend of the family, Maggie, had been contacted by my mum and dad. Anyway, Maggie told my younger brother and me to go with her to her home until my mum and dad got home; so we did. Maggie sent her son, Keith, on to Sayes Court Middle School to meet my elder brother to tell him to go to Maggie's home because my parents had been in an accident. We stayed round Maggie's until my mum and dad got home later that evening.

In the third year of the primary school we all had to choose which middle school we want to go to. I chose to go to St Paul's Middle School, unlike Sandra she chose to go to Sayes Court Middle School, the one my elder brother Stephen went to. That meant Sandra and I were going to separate schools, we were going to be apart, but never mind we were going to see each other at weekends and in the evenings. Luckily for me those two girls, Debbie and Katie, were going to Sayes Court Middle School but unlucky for me so is Sandra.

At the end of Darley Dene Primary School we all had to give in a subject for a book that we all wished for, the subject that I wished for was for 'sowing and knitting' because I had always been interested in 'sowing and knitting'; in fact I have just been shown how to knit by one of my Grandmother's so a book about 'sowing and knitting' will come in handy. Sandra chose a book on 'wildlife', I don't know why because she is not keen on spiders (like me). We were given our books at the last assembly because it lasted longer than normal (they just wanted us to sit on the cold floor for longer, that's all, ha ha).

1981-2

On the first day of starting at St Paul's Middle School, Addlestone, Surrey we all had to go in to the main hall. My mum waited at the side of the hall with all the other parents while us children sat down in the middle of the hall. The headmaster, Mr Spikings sat in a chair at the front of the hall. All the teachers stood behind him. Mr Spikings stood up and introduced himself and the teachers. Then he picked up a bag full of badges with all of our names on them. He called everyone's names out apart from mine, I felt so lost, and he had not called my name out. He asked if everyone had got their badge and I put my hand in the air with tears in my eyes and said 'no I have not got mine sir'. He called me out to the front and looked in to the bag and there in the corner was a little green badge with 'Joanna Norgate' written on it. He pulled it out of the bag and said 'is this your name?' I nodded and he pinned it to my top. I then went and sat down. We then were sorted out in to three classes; we were put in to those classes for the four years of the middle school.

The reason why I had a green badge is because all the pupils were sorted out into four colours: green, yellow, red and blue. All the different rivers: Thames, Bourne, Wye and Mole. I was green for the river Bourne, red was for the river Mole, yellow was for the river Wye and blue was for the river Thames. Whatever your colour you were depended which team you played for on the sports day which was held once a year, I always came last whatever activity I took part in, so I tend to hide in the background when it came to sports day.

I can remember the Christmas that we had that year, it was the biggest Christmas ever. You see my mum and dad went to Black Bush Market which was just past Camberley, which was the biggest market around; well it was the biggest market near us anyway. We never went around there though, I think that is because it was so busy and one of us could easily have got lost (more than likely have been Kevin or I). Anyway, my mum and dad brought black bags full of toys and chocolates, biscuits and that sort of thing. We had a lovely Christmas that year filling ourselves full of chocolates and biscuits.

It was my birthday shortly after Christmas coming into the New Year. On the 18th January I got up early, all of ten minutes because I was born at 6.50am so that was the time I got up. I went down stairs to find my presents and cards all laid out on my chair; wasn't that nice of my mum? I still had thoughts of my Granddad who would have been a year older today if he was still alive, but alas he could not. One present I remember getting for me birthday was a record player, that means that I could borrow my mum and dad's records especially my favourite ones 'The Monkees'. I really do like this group especially the smallest member of the group: Davy Jones. My mum and dad also have Davy Jones's record that he recorded by himself. I really do love them all.

During my time in this school I was in and out of the office from not feeling to well, mainly from a headache or feeling sick or a high temperature. I can remember one time Mr Spikings taking me home but on the way picking my mum up from Sainsbury's in Chertsey, Surrey. That was when she worked there. Another time I can remember I was lying in the chair in the office and the headmaster's office was next door. Well this boy, Jamie Newman, (I can remember his name as clearly as anything, I don't know why?) was taken in to the headmaster's office and Mr Spiking's said to

Jamie bend over. I can still hear the sound of the slipper hitting Jamie's behind to this very day. Mr Spiking's, the headmaster, said to Jamie 'and you can stop that noise or you will get another one'. I felt so sorry for Jamie, I would cry to if it happened to me.

The first year of this school was not in the building; instead it was in huts just outside the school but around the playground. If you wanted to go to the toilet you had to go to the outside ones; it was very cold in the winter especially when the snow came and you wanted to go to the toilet. It was terrible in the winter if the heating had broken down but it was lovely during the summer with all the windows open, it was heaven.

In my first year in this school I can remember doing my family tree during one of my lessons. On this particular day I can remember getting to the part in my family tree of my grandparents and this particular day coming to the stage of my grandfathers. I just began to cry because over the past year I had lost both of my grandfathers, one after the other. The teacher tried to comfort me by taking my out of the classroom away from the rest of the class, this helped a little but nothing could bring back the feelings a had for my grandfathers.

In the summer holidays we went to Selsey Bill which is near Littlehampton, well down that end of the coast. Anyway, we went to the caravan park called the 'White Horse', there are three or four different caravan parks all joined together, our one is the biggest because it is the most popular of the lot. I don't know why it was called the 'White Horse', I still don't know even now.

Our caravan was nicely placed. In our caravan it was an eight birthed (that means it can sleep up to eight people), there was a fridge, cooker, washing machine and in the bathroom there was a shower, a toilet and sink and we even had a key to the toilet/shower block which was just across the road from our caravan. So we were well prepared.

While we were there we made friends with one boy, I cannot remember his name but he was about the same age as my eldest brother, Stephen. Anyway there was one evening when there was a magic show being held in the club house, and this boy wouldn't let them continue until us three got there. How about that for friendship? There was another time when it was the night before we were due to go home, Stephen, Kevin and this boy were playing on these three big tubes going across this dyke. Stephen and this boy got across safely but Kevin suddenly fell in half way across. So Stephen and this boy had to quickly go back and pull Kevin out. Kevin had all smelly mud over his feet and half way up his legs. We took him back to the caravan and my mum went mad because she had packed the suitcases into the car. So she had to unpack the car in order to get the suitcases out to get Kevin some clean clothes. It was not funny for Stephen and me because we got told off for letting Kevin go across the pipes in the first place. And that was the last we saw of this friend.

Also while we were there my mum ran out of frozen peas so she asked my brother Stephen if he would go down to gets some from the shop. Stephen said he had just started a game with Kevin, so I said I would go instead. What a fool I was, I had no idea of the way back, I was alright getting there that was the easy part. I was wandering through what I thought was right way when all of a sudden I realised I was lost. Luckily to my rescue this elderly couple came to mine. They asked me what the matter was. And I told them I was lost. They asked me what number caravan I was staying at, and I told them. They got a map out of all the caravans and looked for the number. Once they found it and took me in their car along with the bag of peas to my awaiting mum and dad. My mum thanked the elderly couple who gladly brought me home to the caravan. I am never going out by myself again, just in case I get lost again!!

1982-3

The second year in the middle school was the best year of my school life because of the teacher, Mr David Bruce. He was the nicest teacher anyone could ever have. He was six foot something high with a beard and the nicest smile. He had the nicest sense of humour and the softest hands. When I first saw Mr Bruce I was so scared of him because of his height but as I got used to him I grow to like him, and do you know what he used to call me? Nutty Norgate, I don't know why. I mean it is not as if I was nutty, I know my maiden name was Norgate at the time, I mean he was saying that all Norgate's are nutty—which is not true!!!

Mr Bruce's classroom was set up of fifteen or so doubles desks to seat us all. At the back of the classroom was a set of sliding doors separating our classroom from the classroom next door. In the middle of the front of the classroom was Mr Bruce's desk; where Mr Bruce sat some of the time. It was in the middle of the set of three classrooms down one side and there were three classrooms down the other side. As you came in to the block of classrooms there was a girls and boys toilets left and right to you. This block of classrooms was separate from the main building, but then it was only a minute walk to get to the main building.

April Fools Day

It was like on April fool's day the whole class wanted to play a trick on Mr Bruce. So first of all we turned the desks around the other way, then we put a Whoopi cushion under Mr Bruce's cushion on his chair and finally we turned his drawers in his desk upside down so that when he opened his draws all his pens and stuff would full out. The Whoopi cushion worked, so did the draws and so did the desks, they all went down with a giggle. Now was Mr Bruce's turn to get his own back. First of all he gave us all a piece of blank paper; the he gave us a 10 pence piece (an old 10 pence piece with the ridges around the side). He then told us to draw around our hand in pencil and then with the 10 pence piece draw a circle around the tips of the hand with pencil. Then with the 10 pence piece go to the top of your forehead run it down to the bottom of your chin. If you have done it right you should have ended up with a line all the way down your face, I know the whole class did; even I did!!

It was in this year that my dad won the 'Milkman of the Year' for his area. For this he got his picture taken and put in the local paper. His picture was put inside of a milk bottle, it looked really good. He also won a holiday for himself and his family to Tunisia for a week. It was fantastic because we had never been abroad before, so we had to make sure we had a passport for the family.

When we got to Tunisia it was night time and all the other 'Milkmen of the Year' for each area all arrived at the hotel. We were not satisfied with the hotel we had. All there was in the room was a bed and a chair, nothing else. I mean would you stay in a room with nothing else but a bed and a chair? So all the milkmen complained and asked to be moved to another hotel, and they did move us. They moved us to an up market hotel called the 'Sinbad Hotel', and it was a five star hotel. It was really nice. It had a separate breakfast bar that was nice, and it had a dinning suite where we sat for our evening meal. One evening my brother Kevin wanted fried egg and chips, but the chef did not know how to cook fried egg so my mum went out in to the kitchen to show the chef how to do it.

One day we all went out for a walk along the sandy road, as we went along we passed a large field full of orange trees and a man was picking them off the trees. Just as I was passing he called me over and offered me an orange, my mum and dad said to me to take it. So I took it, as I did he offered Stephen and Kevin one too. They accepted theirs too. We all said thank you and carried on with our journey. When we got to a big market we were told by our mum and dad 'to not touch anything', so we did as we were told. We had a look around. My mum and dad were the ones who got caught by the shopkeepers when the saying goes 'do not touch unless you are going to buy'. Well my mum and dad touched so they had to buy, the trouble was my dad did not have enough money on him so the shopkeeper's assistance went with my dad back to the hotel to get some more money while my mum and my brothers and I stayed at the shop with the shopkeeper. That was the only trip out we took on that holiday because it cost my parents a lot of money.

There was one thing that I was thankful to Mr Bruce for and that was how to tell the time. It all started off when I got this watch for Christmas one year; it was one of these watches with numbers around the outside. Well I could not tell the time, and at school in a maths lesson it asked a question about the time on a watch. Of course I got it wrong because I could not tell the time, so Mr Bruce kept me and this other girl (who was in the same shoes as me) and went through the basic way of telling the time with us both; and from that day onwards I have been able to tell the time. So thank you Mr Bruce.

There was only one time I was ever told off in class and that was by Mr Bruce, it was for drawing a picture of a little boy and a little girl, I passed them on to a girl a knew called Sarah who was going out who a boy in the class. Mr Bruce found the picture and asked who drew it, I raised my hand and he told me off. I had never been told off before and tears began to form in my eyes. What should I do? I know I had better go to the toilet, as I entered the toilet the tears ran down my face, I just could not let them stop. Eventually they stopped and I washed my face because I had red eyes and tear marks all down my face, after a while I returned to the classroom where Mr Bruce asked if everything was alright, and I replied with a nod of the head.

During the time leading up to Christmas me and my two brothers had to go away to spend a few months with my Aunt and Uncle as my mum was going to spend some time in hospital. This meant us going to school over there. My younger brother Kevin went to the primary school over there; and my brother Stephen went to the secondary school. As for me I went to the middle school with my cousin but I had the choice of years to go into. I could go in to the one of my age or I could go in to the one of my cousin's age (which was a year ahead of me), so I chose to go with my cousin.

School with my cousin was fun because it meant that I didn't actually do the work that they did, it meant that I could help my cousin, if I could! It was like it was her years' turn to do the Christmas Play, and this year they were doing 'Aladdin and the 40 Thieves'. It was a really good play, and I played the back half of a camel, because I was the right height for the hump. My mum and dad came and saw me in the play, and they were both very proud of me. I stayed at this school until Christmas but as soon as school started in January I started back at St Paul's Middle School in Addlestone. I did enjoy myself at my cousins' school but I will enjoy getting back to my own school more.

1983-4

We then left the second year and went up in to the third year, we then had a female teacher called Mrs Dukes, she was a nice teacher but not as nice as Mr Bruce though! In this year we had an extra lesson with a different teacher, a French teacher who obviously teaching us French. French was not my favourite subject, I just could not get the hang of it the way they have their masculine and their feminine words, and it makes it all complicated for me. For this lesson we had to translate our names into French and the teacher could not find a French for my name, Joanna, so she took the French for my mum's English name which is Jacquelyn, so my French name is Jacquelyn (well for this lesson only).

My time spent in the third year was pretty normal for a school life. I did all the usual things a school girl did, normal school lessons: Maths, English, Geography, History, P.E., French, Science, etc. My favourite subject was Maths and my worst subject was French, I don't know why I just can't get the hang of it.

Now was the time I was to start the fourth year of the middle school. The teacher that I was to have was a mature woman called Mrs Plaw; she was one of the teachers that stood no funny business. Mrs Plaw was not a very tall woman in fact she was about five foot tall and she was not a very skinny woman but then again she was not a very large woman. She seemed a very loud outspoken person always in charged but when necessary she can show a bit of kindness. For instance it was coming to the end of a school day and I wanted to go to the toilet very much, we had put our chairs up on top of our desks, like we usually do at the end of school. Then someone started to muck about, which wasted some more time and oh dear I have accidently wet myself. As everyone else left the classroom I stayed behind and went up to Mrs Plaw and said to her that I have wet myself. She was ever so kind; she gave me some clean knickers and a pair of shorts, while she went and cleaned the floor with a mop. That is why I knew the kind side of Mrs Plaw.

Now I am in the fourth year of the middle school we are all allowed to nominate someone to become a 'prefect'. First of all we had to choose a person's, (a boy and a girl) and someone nominated me. I don't know why, because to most of the class I am known as 'cry baby', because if I get told off for anything I cry or sniffle, so I tend to keep in the back ground. I didn't get anywhere in the nominations, I didn't think I would but it was nice to think I was thought of by someone.

A group of us girls from the fourth year got together and formed a football team, now this was 1984 and girls' football was not popular in this time, so we had to really pester the boys' football coach in to setting up a match for us. In the end he set up two games for us, one at home and one away. We lost both, but that doesn't matter it is the experience that matters, well that's what I always say. The first match I played in I played on the forward line and the second match I played in the defence. Both matches I enjoyed playing whatever position I played in but I know what position I didn't what to play in and that is in goal, nobody wanted to play in goal; so poor Emma Jackson who was put in goal to start with was nominated to go in goal for the second time. We all did our best but we lost both games but not by much only by one goal or two.

1984-5

It was time to go to my Secondary School, St Paul's Secondary School. It is a much bigger school than the middle school, but then there are well over a thousand pupils there. I was put in to a class where there was no one from St Paul's Middle School so I was all by myself. There were one or two boys that were from the middle school but no one from my class, so I was all by myself, poor me, I had to make friends with all new faces that was a hard job because they knew each other whereas I didn't know anyone, but I had the next four years to get to know them and for them to know me, even in those four years I still didn't get to know everyone.

Well I got to know quite a lot of people but guess what I even got to know a boyfriend. His name was Timothy Knight. He was a nice boy; I can remember the first kiss I had with him. It seems so funny now but it was a serious kiss then. I had to ask my friend Sandra what sort of kiss I should give him because he was the first serious boyfriend I ever had. It ended up with just a peck on the lips, and then he had to go home. This boy/girlfriend relationship didn't last very long, I don't know why?

I can remember a 'Mufty Day' (this was a day when we could wear whatever we liked to school for a small amount of money, and that money went to the school fund or to another local fund). Anyway, I can remember this 'Mufty Day' because it was my first one so I thought I would dress in my favourite dress which was a red frilly warm looking dress; little did I know it was out of fashion. As I walked into the school building wearing this dress nearly everybody looked at me and laughed. I began to feel so low and I could feel the tears swelling up in my eyes, and it only took one more person to say something nasty about my dress and the tears trickled down my face. And sure enough that one person was just round the corner and the tears came out of my eyes like anything. The lesson I was supposed to be having was Mathematics but I was crying so much the teacher was trying to comfort me and he did. I went the rest of the day ignoring the sniggers and giggles from everyone because I had got used to them by then. But I knew not to wear anything like that dress to the next 'Mufty Day' in future.

1985-6

We spent one year in St Paul's Secondary School then it changed to Abbeylands Secondary School because it mergered with The Meads Secondary School in Chertsey, Surrey. As we changed the name of our school we changed the colour of our school tie but one thing we didn't change was the colour of our school uniform; that stayed as navy blue. We changed our form tutor; that changed to a Mr John Chambers. He seemed a nice fellow; he had fair/ginger hair and was of fair build. Some pupils used to call him 'Flaky' because he had a downdraught problem, but I never joined in because I liked all my teachers.

When I was in registration I notice a poster on the wall advertising 'The Duke of Edinburgh's Award', so I asked Mr Chambers about it and he told me that it was a three level scheme that was for young people aged between 14-25 year olds. The three level schemes were bronze, silver and gold. He mainly dealt with the bronze level. I said that I would be interested in joining. So he filled in a form to get me started. For the bronze award I had to do four things; physical recreation, skill, service and an expedition. For the physical recreation I did archery because it was something that I had always wanted to try and had never had the opportunity to do until now so that is why I chose archery. For skill I did chess because I have been playing chess since I was 7 or 8 and I have always wanted to improve myself up to a level higher than before and I hope that playing chess over this period of time will do it. For service I decided to do the police because I have always been fond of the police force in fact when I am old enough I want to join them. For the service you can do any of the services you wish, such as the police, fire, ambulance etc. As for the expedition on the bronze you have to do a 30 mile hike over two days, spending a night out in a tent and cooking a meal over a camp stove. It is all fun if you have it all planned out correctly and can read a map and use a compass. The expeditions get longer and harder when you go for silver and gold, plus you have to write a journal when you get as far as gold.

It was during a French lesson that I meet him, his name was Timothy Pearce, Tim for short. He was sitting directly in front of me. We hit it of straight away and fell in love, well I thought it was love but who knows.

In the summer holidays I was to get a 'paper round', for the first two weeks of doing the paper round I was to cover the hole of Addlestone, and after that the boy (who took over from my brother Stephen) who is doing the round at the moment comes back from his holiday and the round is big enough to be split in to two. Really the round is big enough to be split in to four but I am not one for saying anything.

It came to the end of the third year and I was playing football with my two brothers out the back of our maisonette when I was tackling the ball with my eldest brother and I hit my hand against the wall, luckily it was my left hand. I couldn't move it, I thought I had broken it, so my mum took me up the hospital and they put it in plaster and told me to come back in a fort nights time to check it to see if it is broken or not. We went back in a fort nights time, luckily for me I had not broken it. So I went in to the school holidays with my left arm in plaster and guess what I started the fourth year with my right arm in plaster; that meant that I couldn't write because at the particular time I was right handed and it was my right hand that was in plaster. What was I going to do? I could practise trying to write left handed, which I did do. So by the time I got my arm out of plaster I could write with both hands but I will probably go back to writing with my right hand.

Back to my paper round, I had a problem I couldn't ride my bike with my arm in plaster, so Molly (the manageress of the shop and a friend of the family) had to hire someone else as well to do the paper round. So I suggested Sandra because I knew she was looking for a job to do. So Molly asked her; and she said 'yes'. So I did the few calls that were way out for them to go to; which was fine for me because when my arm got better that was my new round.

1986-7

How did I break my right arm? You are probably asking? Well it all started with this boy on top of the sheds out the back of where I lived; well he was throwing these little stones at me, so once he got down I decided to chase after him. He was running on grass and turned round the corner; I went to follow and slipped. As I slipped I landed on my elbow and broke both bones straight in half. I called for help to my younger brother Kevin, who came straight away, he told one of his friends to get our mum, who did right away. My mum came and helped me indoors. You could tell straight away that I had broken my arm because it was in the shape of a 'V'. My dad could not take me up the hospital because he is terrible in situations like this; he just goes as white as a sheet, so luckily our next door neighbour Don is always there to take me and my mum up there. When I got up to the hospital the lady on reception said why didn't I call for an ambulance? I don't know what my mum said but I know I was in so much pain.

So I finished the third year in plaster and now I have started the fourth year also in plaster, what a case I am. Everyone started school a week before me, as I was in hospital when school started. I could not wear the proper school uniform as I had my right arm in a three quarter plaster, so I had to borrow one of my mum's tops, one of her navy blue short sleeve tops that was too small for her. As I started a week after everyone else I did not have my timetable written out, so Mr Chambers wrote my timetable out for me. Wasn't that kind of him?

There was one lesson that I could not do and that was CDT: Design and Communication, this was technical drawing and you need two hands to do this kind of drawing, one hand to hold the T-square and one hand to hold the pencil. So instead of doing the drawing by hand I was allowed to do them by computer. Just think this was year 1986 and I am using a new system for technical drawing on a computer, it is brilliant! There were some boys in the class that were jealous of me on the computer that they kept on moaning that they got less of a chance of a go on the computer, it was their own fault!

Another lesson I normally really enjoy is Art, but this particular task I found hard. You see we had this leather tile and this still life model in front of us and we had to cut the model out of the tile with this cutter. I found this really hard to do with one hand, so I had to scrap this idea and the idea that follows with the printing. I think the whole class gave up in the end. Apart from that I really enjoyed this lesson. It was like when everyone else in the art class used to mess around I used to sit in my corner and get on with my work, Mr Gooch noticed this because when everyone else got a detention I didn't, I used to be let off and sent home; it didn't bother me I used to like it. If I remember rightly I think it was Mr Gooch's 21st birthday this year or next year, anyway Happy Birthday to you Mr Gooch.

I found with my lunch times and morning breaks they got so boring, I used to spend most lunch times in with my CDT: Design and Communication tutors (Mr Martin Brown and Mr Trigwell) room making them cups of tea or coffee and of course making myself one as well, that was until I had my chess lesson which was once a week. This chess lesson was part of my Duke of Edinburgh's Award (bronze award) which I was still doing. I was still learning a lot, although it was only supposed to be a twelve week course as

I was still learning a lot Mr Allen (my maths teacher and also my archery teacher) decided to carry on teaching me more.

Three months had passed since I had my arm in plaster and I am free of plaster altogether and I am pleased to be rid of it. The first thing I did when I got home was do some homework in my right hand so that you can read it properly and believe me it looked ever so much more readable than the work done in my left hand.

After I had my arm out of plaster I was coming out of school after it had finished for the day with my friends when in the graveyard there was a fight going on. Someone came running over to me and said that it was between my brother Kevin and a boy called Michael Bennett, well what would you do? I ran over and tried to stop them and this Michael Bennett throws the last punch and it landed right on my nose. The blood poured out everywhere. Michael Bennett realises what he has done and runs away, Kevin asks why did I but in? My friends try to stop my nose from bleeding, and I just head for the school trying to hold my bloody nose.

When I got to the school the receptionist and head of year for year 2 (Kevin's year) dealt with me in the medical room. I told them what had happened. The head of year told me that she would get Michael Bennett to write me an apology letter tomorrow because there is no need for behaviour like that.

The next day at lunch time the head of year for year 2 came up to me and gave me the letter, one thing I did notice was behind her was Michael Bennett, she gave me the letter. I read it; it said that how sorry he was that he punched me and that he will never do it again. I must admit it did say how sorry he was; I said that I did forgive him.

1987-8

The BBC weather man, Michael Fish, made history at the weather this autumn telling the weather; he said there would not be a terrible storm when in fact there was; there was a terrible storm with billions of pounds worth of damages. With the storm going on around us my dad and I slept all the way through it. We could sleep through world war three if it happens.

I started this year of with my 16th birthday; it was on the 18th January. I had passed my Duke of Edinburgh's Award (bronze award) after two years of trying with all those hic-ups mainly with the broken arm(s). We are going to collect our certificates from a school in Stains. But before I was due to collect my certificate I was due to go on my work experience at the local police force during our half term, what a way to spend our half term but I don't mind I'd rather spend my half term doing something creative than spending my time sitting on my backside doing nothing.

This week's work experience for the police was planned out like this:

<u>Monday</u> was to start early in the morning (about 6am) with the police patrol dealing with the motorway (M25) and routes around junction 11 and there a bouts. They also took me around the station and around the headquarters in Guildford. We also popped in to the station in Addlestone (where I am going tomorrow), while we were

there I saw my friend Melanie M who is doing her work experience as well.

Tuesday was a rather boring day even the police officers in the office that dealt with the radios and the main desk both said that the girl that was on there the other day fell asleep half way through. I must admit I did find it a bit boring but I suppose it comes with the job, you have boring days and you have exciting days. The actual job they did today was radio all the vehicles and police officers that were on beat to go to certain places, and if anyone came in to the police station the police officer would see to them; so they played an important roll play to the public which I feel I could play if or when I join the police force.

Wednesday was the day I spent in the Magestraight Courts in Chertsey, Surrey. They were bigger than I expected because I had only been in one, one of the smaller courts, this time I was to spend all my time in the larger court. The police officer I was with was seated to one side so I sat with him; every time the Judges came in and went out of the court we all had to stand up. It was like every time the police officer came in and went out of the court he had to bow because of respect of the judges. There was one case that really interested me and that was one about a school friend who I cannot name her because I said at the time of the hearing that I would not say any name. Anyway this case was about a friend how was taken in a car and was thrown whilst the car was moving. This case was taken to the Crown Court in Guildford, I don't know what the outcome was but I never told the friend that I knew about the case.

Thursday was a frosty morning but that did not stop the police officers from going out on their duty. It was my turn to go out on the beat with one of the police officers. We walked a good ten miles, if not more. On our way round we stopped a car that belonged to a mid-wife, the police officer asked her if she minded if we looked over her car, she said she didn't. So the police officer told me what he would be looking for whilst checking her car, her car was ok. The police officer thanked the mid-wife for her time and saw her on her way. Meanwhile we carried on with his beat. When we got back to the police station it was lunch time so we went for lunch. After lunch the Sargent who was looking after the students, he was giving a talk to a group of teenagers at the private school down the round in between Addlestone and Weybridge, and I was going to go along as a spectator. It was quite fascinating listening to their answers to those questions when those questions are put to us. Afterwards the Sargent and I had to walk back to the station.

That was the end of my work experience week; I must admit it was most enjoyable especially the day on the beat as I enjoyed being out in the fresh air and being out in the open. But I enjoyed all the other days too.

As I said before I went in to my work experience I went to a school in Stains to collect my certificate for my Duke of Edinburgh's Award. As I was waiting to collect my certificate the police Sargent that looked after us on the week of our work experience was there and he recognized me and I did him too. We both said hello and I introduced him to my mum, who had accompanied me along with my grandmother Hoy and Uncle Frank. We only had a short time to chat as we had to go in to collect our certificates. We were the first school to go up because in alphabetical order our school was first: Abbeylands Secondary School.

We had done our mock exams last year (1987) and I have no idea how well or how bad I have done, but I know that I have not done that bad because the teachers would have said something otherwise.

It was a fortnight to go before the final exams are due to start. It was a Friday night and I went to my youth club like I usually do every Friday night, it relaxes me. According to my friends we played volley ball in the church hall. The youth club was run by one of my school friend's parents who belong to this church. The reason why we were playing volley ball in the church hall is because the church hall is deeper than the hall where the youth club is normally held. Anyway, my friends said that we were playing volley ball, they said that I was playing quite well. After wards my dad picked me up at 9.30pm (like usual) and as soon as I got in I got ready for bed as I had to get up for work early next morning. I worked for the bakery down the road (Coombes), behind the counter serving the cakes and bread/rolls and sandwiches. I enjoyed this job so much it was such a responsibility and I respected the manageress, Carol and the staff that worked there all week because they knew everything about the job whereas a was still learning.

Back to that night of me going to bed, I don't remember this but I got out of bed early hours in the morning and went to the toilet/bathroom. My mum asked 'who was that?', but no one answered so she got out of bed. My mum found me lying on the bathroom floor being sick and unconscious. My mum quickly shouted to my dad to call an ambulance Joanna's not well. An ambulance was called and I was taken to our local hospital which was St Peter's Hospital, Chertsey, Surrey. Once we were there I was then looked over and it was diagnosed that it was something to do with the brain; so by this time I was in a coma. The nearest hospital that deals with people with brain problems is in Wimbledon, so I was rushed by ambulance to Adkinson Morley Hospital in Wimbledon. My mum came in the ambulance with me, while my dad came in a car behind with Stephen driving. My younger brother Kevin stayed at home with my Nan Norgate who my dad phoned up before he left with Stephen to come up the hospital early hours this morning.

When I got to the hospital I was rushed to intensive care while my mum was told to wait at the waiting area, she was shortly joined by my dad and Stephen. Stephen sat down and put his socks on which he had not had time to put on before. The first thing that my mum and dad saw when they came in to the intensive care unit was all the wires and tubes; it was not a pretty sight.

While I was in intensive care I was in a coma for two weeks. While I was in this department I frightened my family and friends three times by my heart stopping, but as you can see they have not got rid of me yet because my heart is still beating fast as ever. The only people that were allowed to visit me in the intensive care unit were my mum, my dad and my mum's mum; not my dad's mum. I don't know why something to do with the stupid rules in the hospital that says that the mother's mum is only allowed to visit people in intensive care but the mother of the father is not allowed to visit. But in my case my Nan Hoy let my Nan Norgate in to visit me once or twice. My mum and dad had let the school know how I was getting on, even when my heart had given them a scare three times but they were happy to hear when I was doing well.

After My Stroke

The first thing I remember was when I was in a bed (I had no idea where this bed was or where I was); I went to get out of bed to go to the toilet. As I went to stand I just fell to the floor. I could not stand or walk, HELP!!! What was wrong with me? Why could I not do this simple thing like stand or walk? HELP!!! I had lost my sense of balance. I could not even speak to ask for anything or anyone for help. I could not even cry. Why couldn't I even do that, a simple thing like that; I did not even know my name. What was wrong with me? Why couldn't I even answer these simple questions? HELP!!!

Where am I? What sort of place am I in? HELP!!! I want someone to tell me where I am? What I am? I don't know what I am, who I am? HELP!!!

The next thing I remember was this strange woman walking up the row of beds towards my bed (she was not dressed like the other nurses that looked after me) and sat beside my bed; then she started to talk to me. I did not listen to a word she said, it just went in one ear and out of the other. I had no idea who this woman was (later on I was to learn that she was my mum) but she fed me when it came to meal times as I had not got used to using a knife and folk yet. I had no idea who any of my family was; come to think of it I didn't know I had a family, who were all these people. For a start I had no idea this person who was helping to feed me was my mum, for all I knew she might be a complete stranger to the family. Of course now I know she is my mum and I love her for being there and feeding me.

I learnt that this place that I was in was a hospital (Adkinson Morley) and the time I spent in this hospital I learnt to stand and walk for a little distance with the help of two physiotherapists' but without their help I could not walk a step. I spent two weeks in the main hospital and the one word that I learnt to say was 'yes'. I spent five days out of seven doing physiotherapy, so by the time I was ready to go to the Wolfson Centre (next door to the hospital), I could stand a little by myself but was still in a wheelchair.

The Wolfson Centre was a centre for patients to go to before they went home. When I went to this centre I was pushed over there in a wheelchair as at this time I could not walk, well only steps not distances. When we got in there we went in to a lift and down a floor and along a corridor then into this room with two beds and two basins in it. It also had a built-in wardrobe with two doors with two locks in them. There were two wooden chairs; I had the choice of beds, so I pointed to the one next to the window, as this had a lower bed than the other one and that is what I liked, a nice low bed.

After I had settled into my room I went upstairs in my wheelchair in the lift and around the corner to the rest room, where everyone went after they had done all their different activities for each day before they went for their tea.

One person I met when I first went in to the Wolfson Centre was Nurse Joe, he was like a giant compared to me. He must have been at least 6 foot 6 inches, with long hazel brown hair tied back. I liked this nurse because he was friendly and kind that was what I liked about a place like this, there was not a horrible nurse or doctor anywhere in sight.

I met some of the patients while I was there, one was this man his name was John Gunn. My dad had a nick name for him, 'Ben Gunn'. He was a slim man with short brown hair. He was in there because he was involved in an accident with a police car. The police officer opened the car door while John was going past on a bicycle. He was such a funny fellow to be around always laughing and joking about himself. Another was Bert. He was in his 50's. He was a kind man because he used to push me around the centre, until he left the centre to go home. Another was Richard. He was a tall, tubby man with a beard.

Before Bert left to go home all the other inmates that were going to leave at the same time as him asked if they could hold a bar-be-q to show their thanks for all their hard work, so they did this on one Friday afternoon after they had finished all their classes. My parents and brother, Kevin, were allowed to stay for the bar-be-q. Kevin enjoyed himself because he could help himself to as much as he could eat, I could only manage two hot dogs as I am not a very big eater.

After Bert left Richard started to push me around the centre grounds. This I didn't mind at first because it was alright, but then he began to push me around outside. When Richard pushed me around outside he used to take me to a certain place and assault me. He used to put his hand down my top and play with my left breast. This happened five days a week for three weeks. I never told anyone about this as all I could say was 'yes', even if I wanted to say 'no'. The only way I could let anyone know if I wanted to say 'no' is to shake my head. That is one thing that will haunt me until I die. The only way I could get away from him is to walk, so I was more determined than ever to walk.

I spent about five months in this centre. I used to go home at weekends, Friday evenings to Sunday evenings. One Friday evening I had a school certificate evening to go to. This was to give everyone their certificates for their final examinations. I did not take any of my exams because I was ill in hospital, so they passed me on six out of nine of my exams because the based my grades on my mock examinations and my course work. The reason why they did this was because I was in the first year (1988) to take the GCSE examinations. The grades I got are as followed:

English (D)
English Literature (D)
General Science (C)
Home Economics (Child Development) (F)
Art and Design (E)
CDT: Design and Communication (D)

As you can see that the subject I got the best grade for was General Science, but this was one of my worst subjects. My best subject was CDT: Design and Communication because that was technical drawing which I really enjoyed. The only subject I would have liked to have got an examination grade for was Mathematics, but I was one piece of course work short. The other two subjects that I did not get a grade for were French and Social & Political Studies. I did not mind as I was not much good at either of these subjects.

Anyway back to that evening out. All the pupils' names were put into groups. It was time for me to get into position, my friend Melanie T helped me as I found it difficult to walk. Melanie T is a nice person, she is a nice friend who is taller than me; mind you everybody is taller than me. It was my turn to go onto the stage to get my certificate but first I had to go up a small flight of stairs. As I began to climb up the stairs with Melanie's help everyone started to clap at me as we went on. I could not understand why they were clapping but as I got my certificates instead of shaking my hand the important gentleman just gave me my certificates and joined in with everyone else and clapped. So I then turned to go off the stage with Melanie's help. After all the certificates were given out there was some refreshments, I did not want to stay as I was feeling so tired as this was the latest I had been up for a long time. Before we left a few of my teachers came up to me and said how glad they were to see me, shortly after we left.

While I was at the Wolfson Centre the activities I did were Physiotherapy and Speech Therapy. I did the Physiotherapy three times a day for five days a week and the Speech Therapy once a day for five days a week. The Physiotherapy was hard work but I enjoyed doing some of the activities they got me doing, like standing up kicking a ball with my right foot or standing on my right foot and kicking the ball with my left foot, that was harder than kicking the ball with my right foot. I enjoyed doing this especially when the ball went all the way down the corridor and the physiotherapist had to go and get it. Another thing I used to like doing in the Physiotherapy was walking up and down the stairs they had in one of the gyms. I did not like the speech therapy because it was hard work trying to speak because it gave me a headache. One time it hurt my head so much that it gave me a bad migraine that lasted for three or four days. It was so bad that they had to transfer me back to the main hospital for two days until it eased off.

While I was in the Wolfson Centre I had my right leg/ankle in plaster. Don't worry I did not break it; it was to straighten my right ankle and foot because they were bent because of the stroke. Mind you it was not on there that long, not even a day. I just could not bear it on there much longer than that. It hurt me so much, the pain from my ankle I had to have it taken off. So Nurse Joe came and took it off for me in the middle of the night. What a pain I am!

At weekends I used to leave the Wolfson Centre to spend time at home with my family (at least I think this is my family), I am still getting used to all the different members of my family, such as my two nan's, and all my different aunts and uncles. During one week my favourite Uncle Martin and Aunt Brenda (I think that they are my favourite Uncle and Aunt, that's what my mum said anyway) came up to visit me, it was a nice surprise. On the way up they saw notices for the circus to be shown at Woking and the wondered if I would like to go? So they asked my mum and she said 'yes', without even asking me; but I didn't mind as I can't remember the last time I saw a circus. All I can remember is seeing the animals, clowns etc. But I expect it has all changed now because they have not got all the animals; it is a shame. So my Uncle Martin paid for my mum, my dad, my younger brother Kevin and me to go to see the circus.

I was right when I said that the circus had changed, it was not like what I remember seeing it like with clowns, tigers, lions, elephants, horses, etc. But this circus had clowns, an elephant and a couple of horses apart from that it was just people doing different acts. Apart from not seeing the tigers and other animals I thought it was quite a good circus.

It was like another weekend I can remember my Uncle Martin and Aunt Brenda came up to my home to pick me up to take me to their home in Henfield, West Sussex. We had a great weekend, as they lived near Brighton we spent one day down there, me in the wheelchair and my Uncle Martin, Aunt Brenda and my two cousins Claire and Phillipa walking beside me. We went in to see the dolphins; that was great because the girls hadn't seen them until now and I had never seen them either; so it was a surprise for all three of us. It was a shame that the weekend had to come to an end but as the saying goes 'all good things come to an end'.

One day back at the centre, I have moved my bedroom to the ground floor, which is three floors down from the ground floor. Anyway, I left my wheelchair by my bed and walked up six flights of stairs to breakfast, it took me some time but I managed to do it. After breakfast I walked around to the physiotherapy rooms. Later, I walked around to the speech therapy room for my speech lesson. Some days it is so hard especially for someone who is trying to learn how to speak and finding it so hard to say the simple words let alone the long words. But I was getting the hang of walking, but at the end of the day I was tired but I was getting there. From that day onwards at the centre I walked to and from the therapy rooms. The only time the wheelchair came out was when I was at home at weekends.

After being at the Wolfson Centre for what seemed like forever but it was only five months, I was allowed to go home. My dad came to pick me up. On the way home we stopped at the local wheelchair centre, in Chertsey, Surrey, to get me a wheelchair for my permanent use, even though I was walking around the centre my mum wanted to get me a wheelchair, I don't know why, I wanted to walk everywhere but my mum knows best.

My walking was coming along with leaps and bounds, but I wish I could say the same for my speaking. I had to go up to my local hospital once a week (Wednesdays') to see their Speech Therapist. My dad took me up there when he finished work. While I was out with my dad he used to encourage me to talk but as soon as we got back home my mum used to tell me to sit down and shut up because she was watching television. So I was even longer in the speech department, instead of being able to talk in about six months it took me about two years or longer in some cases.

It was the same with the physiotherapy I had to do at home, when I went to do my right leg, my right hand and arm exercises my mum used to tell me to stop doing the hand exercises because she wanted to either dish up the dinner or for some other reason, so I had to stop. It was like every morning my mum used to push me up the road to do the shopping. One morning I asked my mum if I could walk up there, she said 'No because she didn't have time to wait for me'. So I never asked her again. How unfair! I love you really mum.

My friend Melanie T used to come round two or three times a week, after she had finished work. She works for the Post Office. We used to walk (I hobbled) down the road to look around the shops and we also popped into the local Social Services to see our friend David Baines. He was a Senior Social Worker. He always had time to see us. We used to talk about anything and everything. David Baines used to ask me questions and I tried my best to answer them. Melanie T used to walk with me to our secondary school; we used to go up there to see a few of the teachers who were always pleased to see how well I was doing.

It was Christmas 1988 and I thought I had heard the last of Richard (from the Wolfson Centre). When out of the blue he telephoned me. After he had finished speaking to me, I felt so sick inside because of the things he had done to me and the things he had just said which were horrible. I have never told anybody about what had happened, as far as I was concerned that was in the past and it is the future I am looking for and PLEASE let this be the last of what I am going to hear of Richard.

1989

At the age of seventeen I went to the local college in Weybridge, Surrey on a one day per week scheme (Monday). When I went there I used to do a sort of English lesson in the morning and a cooking lesson in the afternoon. I went there for about six months. During the lunch breaks I sometimes went and met up with my best friend Sandra. I only saw her for about twenty minutes because it took me about 15 minutes to walk to the huts I used to work in. I can remember doing a Dundee Cake that cost me £3.00. I can remember meeting a boy there, his name was Andrew. He gave me his name and address; it was a place in Woking. I really like this boy, he is nice.

At this age I had to go into hospital up at Sheffield for some treatment that I did not know about it, all I know is I am going to have some sort of treatment. It was a very large hospital, at least nineteen floors. At the time I had no idea why I was going to this hospital. I was to stay in this hospital for three nights and four days. My Uncle Frank took us (my mum, my dad, Kevin, my Nan Hoy, her dog Brandy and me) up to Sheffield in his car. We left early Monday morning, about 2am. We arrived there about 10am. My Uncle Frank took my parents to a B&B, where they were going to stay before we went to the hospital.

When we got to the hospital we had to wait in the waiting room for about 30 minutes before I was taken to my bed. I was shown to this side ward where there were five other women and this other empty bed which was shown to me. There was only one woman in there that was kind enough to say hello to us, and her name was Dorothy. She was a middle aged woman, very slim with brown hair. Out of the five women she was the only one that was kind enough to talk to me throughout my stay in that hospital, and I am thankful for that. That evening she asked my mum for my address, my mum gave it to her and she gave my mum hers. I only stayed in this ward for two nights as they did the treatment in another part of the hospital.

On the second day the doctor who was going to give me the treatment came up to the ward where I was to see my mum, my dad and me, to tell us about the treatment. The doctor told us what was going to happen (I did not take it all in because I did not understand it all). The doctor decided it was best that we saw what was going to happen to me instead of just talking about it, so we went down and out of this part of the hospital and walk a little way (seemed like forever to me, but only a short distance for a normal person) until we got to another part of the hospital. When we got inside of this part of the hospital we went down, yes down in the lift in to the basement and along a corridor into a room where there was a machine. This machine looked like a long bed coming out of a big dome. The doctor said that I was going to have a brace fitted to my head so that they could fix this machine correctly to me head so that the radiation treatment could be correctly transmitted to my head. At the time I still was not sure what was going on, but I do now. After the doctor had showed us this machine he took us back to the main hospital. Once we got there the doctor said that I was allowed to go out of the hospital with my parents, so we went around the town of Sheffield. We went round the shops and had something to eat out because the doctor said that I could. It was about 3pm when I got back to the hospital because I was feeling very tired, and I wanted to lie down and have a sleep. So my parents left me at the hospital to sleep while they went to their B&B.

The next day, Wednesday, I was not allowed any breakfast as I was to have my treatment. I was given two tablets (along with my normal medication) to make me drowsy. The next thing I remember was being slightly awake, and all these people in blue gowns around me. I felt a burning sensation around my groin. The next thing I remember was having these small screws drilled into my head, it was a brace being screwed into my skull, and it felt so heavy. The next thing I knew I was being pushed on this bed into an awaiting ambulance to take me to this other part of the hospital.

I arrived at the other part of the hospital in about five minutes. I was taken down to the basement where that machine was. The reason why I had the head brace on was because they had to screw my head into position so that they could get the right spot/brain haemorrhages, so that the radiation treatment went in the right place. This took about an hour. I can remember that someone said to me that I was about the thirty-third person in this hospital to have this treatment done.

After this had taken place I was on my way up to the ward in this part of the hospital, when the lift opened on the ground floor and my parents got into the lift as well. They said hello but I did not want them to see me in this state (they had taken the brace of my head now, I looked a right state), but my parents did not listen to me. I was a mess, where the head brace had been attached to my head/skull, I had bleed quite a bit that my hair was all mangled together that it looked all knotted together but it was not, and I had blood all down the back of my head, and had gone into my hair. My hair looked a right state, all tangled up.

Later on when my parents left and I still felt a little drowsy, I wanted to go to the toilet. I got out of the bed with a struggle and out of the side room I was in. I then asked a nurse that was about where the toilet was, she quickly hurried over to me and said that I should not be out of bed. She helped me to the toilet, and then helped me back to bed. She then gave me the buzzer for the next time I wanted something, and then left. I then fell asleep and did not awake until my mum and dad came up to visit me later the evening.

The following day I was discharged from the hospital. My parents and I made our way to the railway station, and then got on the train to Victoria, in London. On the train we had seats booked because it was a long journey. When we got to Victoria, in London, my dad went ahead to find my Uncle Frank, my Nan Hoy and Kevin. My mum and I followed behind slowly, as I was a slow walker and I was feeling very uneasy. I think it has something to do with the treatment I had the day before. We then drove home back to Addlestone. I went to bed as soon as I got in because I was very tired, as it had been a very stressful day.

The following day, I got out of my bed and made my way down stairs. When I got down the bottom of the stairs I walked into the kitchen and said to my parents that my face was feeling all swollen and I was feeling sick. My mum said to me, go back to bed and it will be alright. So my dad helped my back upstairs and into my bed, where I soon fell asleep. A couple of days later, I found out that I had radiation treatment up at Sheffield and that was the only place in England that did that sort of treatment at the moment.

A week or so later I felt better. Melanie T came round to see how I was, and asked if I was ready to go out for our usual walk. I said yes, but my mum was a bit cautious about me going out but she let me go anyway.

As we walked up the road we took it nice and slowly, as I was feeling a bit uneasy because this was the furthest I had been for well over a week. We decided to go and see our friend David Baines. We were greeted like friends do. David Baines asked me what I was going to do now that I have finished going to college. I said that I didn't know. He asked what me what my interests were. I said anything to do with office work apart from answering telephones. Then he had an idea about going to Egham Rehabilitation Centre. I said ok. So we filled in the forms and sent them off. I went home and told my mum what I had done, I don't think she was too pleased with what we had done but what was done was done.

A few days later I received a letter from the rehabilitation centre. It said that I had to go there for a week to see what sort of work they thought I would be good at. I showed David Baines the letter and he was pleased that I got in so soon. My mum was not happy about me going to Egham as it was a residential place. David Baines said that in some cases they do allow the person to travel there each day, and I would be one of those people. This made my mum feel a bit better.

It came to the day I went to Egham. I got up, washed and got dressed ready to go. The taxi came and I went to the rehabilitation centre. It was a large place, bigger than I expected. I had to wait in the reception for about ten to twenty minutes, I was not alone, there was about five other people waiting there too. Eventually this gentleman came and introduced himself to us. He told us to follow him, so we all did. I did my best to keep up. We walked throw the work shop where other disabled people of all disabilities were working. In the bottom left hand of the work shop were two rooms and beyond that were some seats. We were all shown to the seats and told to sit down until called. We were then taken one at a time and were given all these tasks to do. I did all right; I could do almost all of them. The only one I found difficult was the one where you needed two hands in holding the strip of plastic and putting it round the pegs that were sticking out of the machine to make a coat hanger. As the man said there are certain things people find easy and some hard. This lasted for four days, it was supposed to last for five days but we all finished the work early. After the course had finished I was sent another letter asking if I would like to go back for an eight week course to improve my skills, I said yes. I was due to go back there in the October and that is when my life changed once again.

October came

I got the taxi to the rehabilitation centre, which I did every morning and it picked me up every evening, just as before as my mum did not want me to be a residential client there, although I cannot blame her as I would not want to stay away from home. I managed to arrive there safely by taxi despite what the weather was like. I walked into the reception and introduced myself to the man on reception. He told me to take a seat and someone will be along shortly. As I sat down I noticed someone else, it was a coloured woman. I can remember her name, Norma. We were both going to the same place of work. That was where they did office work, answering telephones etc. As we went into this large room, I noticed a young man working and he looked at us too. We were shown to two desks and were talked to telling us what we were going to do over the next seven/eight weeks we were there. As we were working that young man I noticed working came over and started talking to Norma, and then he turned to me and asked me what my name was? I said 'Joanna, but I prefer to be called Jo'. He said his name was David.

Later that day David went out of the room that we were in, then a few minutes later he came back in and came over to me. He said that they wanted me in the office along the corridor. So I went with him as I did not know where the office was and David did. I walked into the office behind David; then the ladies in the office said that they did not want me, so we walked back to the room. On the way back David said that he knew that the ladies did not want me, and that he just wanted to get me by myself to talk to me. I was flattered as I have never been taken back like this before, I was touched. I walked (hobbled) as fasted as I could back to the room we were working in because I did not want David to see me blushing as much as I was. I don't know what the matter with me since I have suffered with my stroke I seemed to blush easily. And this was one of those occasions.

There was one afternoon when we finished for the day. When we were going out of the room we had to clock in/out by putting a card with our names on it into a machine. I was just going out of the door when there was this young girl waiting for someone. This girl had Down's syndrome; it was the first time I had ever come across anyone with this condition before. She asked me if David Barnes had come out yet. I replied that I didn't know, and carried on walking to catch my taxi home. Little did I know that this David Barnes was this young man David.

Over the few weeks David always spoke to me and I spoke back as best as I could. On David's last day he asked me for my name and address, so I gave it to him and he gave me his. This other fellow also asked me for my name and address. I felt so rotten afterwards because I gave him a made up address. I am so sorry but I did not like the look of this fellow that is why I gave him a mock address. Now I think about it I wish I had given him my real address but it is to late now. If this fellow gets to read this book I am sorry for giving you the wrong address so please email my address at the end so we can keep in touch.

The very next day I received a letter in the post, it was from David. I couldn't believe it, someone writing to me, is my luck changing? I took it to Egham and showed it to Norma. She was a bit jealous because she hadn't got one. That made my day; I really thought my luck had changed.

I soon sent one in the post, but as soon as I got one in the post another one turned up. It seemed that for everyone I posted two or three would arrive. I was beginning to get annoyed with all this, especially seeing as I didn't know what to say three quarters of the time, but I know one thing I did say was that if he wanted anything to come between us he had to give up smoking and do you know he gave up just for me.

I have kept all my letters that David has sent to me and the same for I sent David. It is like I have kept most of my diaries since I have suffered a stroke. I even kept all the newspaper cuttings that concern me when I first suffered a stroke; it has my school photograph which could have been better.

Also in 1989, my social worker friend, David Baines offered me a job but he was not sure how much I was allowed to earn. So my mum phoned someone up that deals with finances and they said I was not allowed to earn anything but I could do it on a voluntary bases. So my mum telephoned David Baines up and told him what the finance people had said. So I went to work (on a voluntary bases), but David Baines gave me £15 a day for turning up. The work I did was sorting out all the files, but I was not alone I was working with another lady (I cannot remember her name); anyway we were to sort all these files into categories such as different dates, whether the person is blind/partially sighted, whether the person was a child being abused etc. But this job would not be starting until the New Year, which was fine with me.

1990

It was my birthday on the 18th January, but I was having my 18th birthday party on the 6th January instead. I was inviting all sorts of people, such as John Chambers (my form tutor from school), Andrew (that boy I met from college), Tim (an ex-boyfriend from secondary school), David Baines (my social worker friend), all my school friends and the rest was family. I did not invite David (who I met from the rehabilitation centre) because I did not think he would be able to come. Tim had a bit of an accident in one of the dances, he opened his legs a bit too much and split his trousers. Luckily enough we only live 5 minutes away so Stephen lent him a pair of his. For my birthday my Nan Hoy made my birthday cake, the trouble was she made the icing so hard it was almost impossible for me to cut it, but I managed with a little help.

I got five black bags of presents and cards, some of the cards had money inside of them; so I had a double surprise when I opened them as well. Most of the present were jewellery but there were some chocolate in there too. Plus I had some more presents to come from my close family (my mum and dad) on the 18th January, which I could not wait for.

My Nan Hoy and Uncle Frank took me out on the 17th January to buy my birthday present. We looked round all the clothes stores until I saw a coat, it was one of those rain macs that was in the fashion at that time; but when I saw the price I went and looked at something else but my Nan said if that mac was what I liked then they would get it for me, and they did. Guess what the price was? Nearly £100, and in those days that was expensive. But I was over the moon with this present that my Nan and Uncle had brought me.

Today was my 18th birthday on the 18th January and I was lucky to be here after what I had been through. Today I got the rest of my presents from the rest of my family. Of my Nan Norgate I got a jewellery box to put some of the jewellery in that I got from my birthday party. I was not expecting anything else of my Nan Hoy but I got a typewriter. Plus a few other presents.

By now I was getting used to having to share Melanie T with Stephen, seeing as they were falling in love with each other. One day she would come round for Stephen the next it would be for me, I would not know where I am with her spending all this time around here.

On the 30th January I started my first day of voluntary work with David Baines (my social worker friend); we started off by driving to pick up some cork for a notice board for his offices. Then we drove back to his offices to sort out what we were to do about these files. I went to work twice a week to do the files. I really enjoyed working with one of the other ladies while doing the files. Today was also Melanie T birthday; just think about it having a school friend for a sister, it will be fun!!!

David was still writing to me as often as before, in fact he has started at the Queen Elizabeth Training College in Leatherhead for a short spell. I asked my mum if he could come for dinner one Sunday, she said yes. So I invited him to come on February 18th. I sat on the fence outside our place waiting for him to come; and he just walked straight passed me. He didn't even recognize me, not until I spoke to him and said 'that's it just walk straight pass'. And he turned and said 'sorry I didn't even recognize you'. I took him in and introduce him to my family, they all liked him. Later on David and I went for a walk down to our local park and while we were out I became his girlfriend and he became my boyfriend. When we got back my dad said he would take David back to the college as it was a residential college and it was getting a bit late for David to catch the trains back to Leatherhead.

David came over to my home in Addlestone on a regular basis at the weekends and on the 24th March we went to Guildford. We were going to go to Woking but my mum wanted to come along, so we said we were going to Guildford while she went to Woking. When we got there it was drizzling so we didn't hang about, we went straight to Argus. We went over to the 'jewellery' cabinet and looked at the rings. David pointed at one and I said yes, and they did it in my size too which is a size 'J'. David also looked at the earrings and saw some crystal hearts. After he had paid for them we both felt a bit hungry, so we went to the McDonald's round the corner. We got our meal and went upstairs to sit down; the only place to sit was on this double table next to this middle aged couple, so we sat there. As we were eating David pulled out this ring and said to me 'Jo will you marry me?' And I said 'Yes of course I will'. And the middle aged couple sitting next to us said 'congratulations', and that is when David proposed to me in McDonald's.

On the bus on the way home I felt a bit sick so we decided to get off the bus in Sheerwater, and as soon as I got off the bus sure enough I was sick. We thought it was due to travel sickness because I suffer from travel sickness on buses/coaches. We got on another bus a little way down the road and managed to get home. When we got home the first person I showed my new ring to was my Nan

Hoy, she was very pleased for us both. My mum was happy too, in her own way.

We told my mum about me being sick she said it was properly my appendix playing up. She took me down to the local surgery to see the local doctor just to get it checked out. The local doctor said the same thing as my mum. So I went back home. Later that evening about 9.30pm I was rushed to hospital with appendicitis, which almost burst. I was in hospital for four days in all.

While all this was happening David was at college at Leatherhead worrying his mind out, the poor thing. He did visit me while I was in hospital, one of his friend's from college drove him over so he could visit me; wasn't that sweet of him? This episode was too much for David it made him starts smoking again, I couldn't blame him but I hope he stops soon though.

My mum, my dad, my younger brother and I used to go over to Leatherhead to the Queen Elizabeth Training College so that I could see David, oh and so my mum could play their game of bingo. David used to call the numbers out because he used to do it for a local business in the town he comes from, Folkestone, Kent.

It was Thursday 12th April when David and I went down to Folkestone to visit David's flat. It is the first time that I have ever been away from home since my stroke, well that is by myself anyway. We got off the train and into a taxi at the station, we then arrived at 5 Harvey Place late in the evening, so I did not get a look at the place; but it looked nice at what I could see. The next day, Friday 13th April, was a nice surprise for me; it was the day I lost my virginity on his living room floor. It was funny, David said 'Tell me if this hurts and I will stop'. I said 'Ouch that hurt, but try again'. And he did, but this time it didn't hurt and that's how I lost my virginity.

It was like on several trips down to Folkestone I had to spend several trips to the William Harvey Hospital, Ashford, Kent with concussion (as my head was very fragile at this time due to the radiation treatment I had the previous year) mostly due to the fault of David and his wicked way with his sense of humour. The first time was both of our faults because we were both mucking about on the bed, David was tickling me I jumped back and banged my head against the bedroom wall and knocked myself out cold. The second time we were sitting face to face on the arm chair in David's living room when I leant back to far and banged my head on the floor and knocked myself out cold. These are just two of the many different cases that there are. They got to know me quite well up at the William Harvey Hospital.

There was David's Aunt Jenny and Uncle Roger who lived up Plain Road in Folkestone, with their Jack Russell dog named Wendy, who we often visited. I used to tease the dog, Wendy, with my chocolate biscuit by waving it about in the air before eating it, and this used to really torment her especially when in the end I ate it all and didn't give her a drop of chocolate. They are religious people and very much into music, any sort, I say any sort a part from heavy metal.

We even visited David's sister Chris and her husband Phil and their family in Harlow, Essex. One particular time we went up to their house to house sit and look after the dog. We were sleeping in their double bed when we heard the whole family leave. As we heard the front door shut David decided he wanted some breakfast (not the sort you can eat but the sexual type of breakfast), so David went underneath the covers for his breakfast. Unknown to us Chris had come back in for her passports; she forgot that they were in her bedside cabinet. She came in and David was still down underneath the covers. Chris just laughed and I went bright red with embarrassment, while David just stayed under the covers.

Chris told the rest of the family and we got taken the micky out of from the rest of the family when they came back home.

On our visit down to David's flat we also visited an old lady, Margaret. She was a nice lady; while David was at home she had him doing odd jobs about the home for her, like painting all her up-stairs for her because she had not been up there for years. To me she was like a third Grandmother. You see she had no children of her own because she had never been married because she spent all her life in service, even when she got old she carried on working. I often did her dusting for her and I put things back exactly where they came from, that was one of the things she learnt when she worked. We also met his Aunt Jenny and Uncle Roger there because they popped in there for their tea. They are a nice couple.

One of David's closet friend's is Victor Smith, he is a gay man; that is the sort of friend that anyone could have. I mean he is the truer as a friend can be. Victor has recently met another gay friend named Raymond, who he is very fond off; even though there is a big age gap between them both. Raymond is only a few months older than me, and there is a 30 year gap between Victor and me. But we all get along as a group despite our age gap.

We spent quite a few weekend breaks down at Folkestone. My mum, my dad and Kevin used to come down by train on a Sunday, just for the day though. Sometimes my Nan Hoy and Uncle Frank used to come with them; because my Uncle Frank used to work for the railway and used to get free tickets.

On the 3rd August David and I were going down to Folkestone to spend a fortnight down there because David was due to do his work experience at the local newspaper place.

We telephoned my mum up from David's and she suggested that I telephoned Richard (from the Wolfson Centre) up, because he lived in Dymchurch; that was just down the road from Folkestone. We telephoned Richard up; little did David know about the time before in the centre next to the Adkinson Morley Hospital, Wimbledon. We arranged to meet up together on the Thursday (two days' time) evening as David was out during the day on his work experience.

On the Thursday 7th August David left at 9am to go for his work experience. At 9.30am the buzzer went on the intercom, I thought it was David; I thought he had forgotten his keys or something but instead it was Richard. Like anyone would have done, I let him in. He came up. I opened the door and let him in. He was a large man (in size) and in built. He had a big beard that made him look like a builder. As he came in he sat down on the stall next to the breakfast bar. I asked him whether he would like a cup of tea or coffee. He replied 'Yes a cup of coffee'. So I made him a cup of coffee like he requested. I then sat in the arm of the armchair. Richard then said 'How about a kiss to say hello then?' So I gave him a kiss on one of his hairy cheeks, just to say hello, then I went to sit down but he wouldn't let me go. Instead he put his left arm around me so I could not move. With his right arm he managed to get my top off me and take my bra down my waist. He then started to kiss my left breast and then started to bite my left breast. The more I tried to get away the more he held on. Then to my relieve David came in and Richard let go. I ran past David into the bed room, leaving David to sort Richard out in the other room. I heard David say to Richard in a calm voice, 'I think you had better go'. And with that Richard left. David came into the bedroom and saw me there shaking.

In the bedroom David asked if I was alright. I replied 'No'. He told me to stay where I was because he was going to call the police. He was gone for what seemed a long time but it was only ten minutes.

They arrived just a few minutes after that. It was two policewomen that came; one was called WPC Sue Austin. They told me to tell them everything that had happened. So I told them everything, even what had happened two years previously at the Wolfson Centre. David was shocked, he had no idea what had happened before. The policewomen were there about two hours, writing down everything. They then left saying that someone would be round Richard's house as soon as possible to arrest him.

They also suggested David took me to see his doctor to get me checked out for bruising around the left breast. So David took me to see his local doctor. While we were in the waiting room David noticed a number on the notice board and got up and asked the receptionist if she had a pen and paper he could borrow, she gave them to him. He wrote down something, I am not sure what. Anyway it was time for us to go into see the doctor. David told the doctor what had happened, then the doctor turned to me. He asked me if I minded if he touched my breast. I said 'I did not mind', because I knew David was there. The doctor said there were some signs of bruising around the teeth marks but apart from that nothing serious. David said about me sleeping tonight, would I have problems? I said 'Yes, I would'. So the doctor gave me some very weak sleeping tablets. After that we left.

That left me in a bit of a mess. I didn't know what to do with myself. I couldn't stay in that flat. He took me to a bench that was near a telephone box and told me to sit there, which I did. While David went to the telephone box and telephoned someone, I don't know who? All he told me when he got back was that someone was coming shortly to help me, and sure enough in about 30 minutes time someone did come.

This tall thin man, with a beard and long blonde hair came walking up to us and held out his hand and said 'Hello, my name is Andy'. Andy then asked if there was anywhere we could talk. David said that there was his flat just around the corner, I quickly said no, because I didn't want to go back to that flat. So David said hang on I will telephone his Aunt Jenny and see if we can go up there. That left me alone with Andy for a few minutes, and Andy started talking but before I could answer David came back with good news, his Aunt's place is free so we can chat there all evening if we wanted.

So Andy drove us up to Aunt Jenny's place, which is a lovely place. When we went into Aunt Jenny's house we were greeted by her Jack Russell, Wendy. David went into the kitchen to make us all a cup of tea while Andy and I sat down and began to chat. I began to tell Andy about Richard and what had happened, he listened to it all. We were there for about two and a half hours. After all the chat we had come to the conclusion that we were going back to David's flat.

David went into his flat first followed by Andy and then I slowly went in after. The cup of coffee I made Richard was still sitting on the side. It had gone cold; the milk had gone cold on top and had separated from the coffee. David had got hold of the cup and poured it down the sink, and threw the cup in the bin. It was one of David's favourite cups. Andy asked if I had his name and address in my address book, I replied 'yes'. So I got my address book out, and turned to his name and address. Andy then asked if I had anyone else's name and address I wanted to keep. I said 'yes', so I copied down their names and addresses. After that Andy ripped out Richard's name and address and I watched him burn it. We did some more talking and we decided to go over to Lydd, Kent to where David's mother, Joan Allen and step-father, Ron Allen lived. Andy said that he would take us, and we said thank you. So David packed a bag with our clothes in because he was not sure how long we were staying over at his mum's.

Over at Lydd, David phoned my mum up to tell her what had happened. I would not speak to her as I did not talk to anybody because I felt so guilty for what had happened, I felt it was my fault, I felt as though I let him do it to me. I felt so ashamed for what had happened. When in fact none of it was my fault at all, I did not let him do this to me he help himself, he forced himself into my space, my private space. It took a couple of days before I spoke to my mum; she was all sympathetic, which is unusual for my mum.

I spent quite a few times in the William Harvey Hospital, Ashford Kent, this year that the nurses in casualty seemed to know me be sight rather than by name.

I came down to David's flat quite a few times since that incident. On one occasion David went and brought two tickets to see Des O'Conner. Neither of us had ever seen him live before, so it would have been a surprise for both of us.

We enjoyed the show very much; I would recommend his show to anyone. After the show had finished David had arranged it for us to see Des behind the stage. I couldn't believe my luck, and to go with it Des gave a red rose and he gave me three kisses on the left cheek; but before he kissed me he asked if it was alright if he could because David had told them about the incident that had happened and I said 'yes it was', because I knew David was there and because Des looked nothing like what Richard looked like. We had a late night that night, about 1am, so we had a late morning next morning.

1991

On Wednesday February 6th was the court case about the assault. I was at home in Addlestone and my mum came with me. We travelled from Addlestone to Maidstone in Kent where the case was being held. Our train was a little bit late, but what do you expect from British Rail. At Maidstone station we went to catch a taxi and there was this other woman there also wanting to catch a taxi to Maidstone Crown Court so we shared the same taxi.

When we arrived at Maidstone Crown Court it was a beautiful building. David was already at the courts waiting for us to get there. He came out of the court as soon as we got out of the taxi. I had my white stick with me because I am partially sighted in my right eye. Inside the court it has got the magnificent marble stair case that leads up to the courts. Inside we were led by someone who works with the ushers who takes you where you need to go; anyway we were taken to where the police officers wait until they are called.

We were there forever, but my mum went ahead to the court room to listen to what was happening. She was gone for a long time. About 3 hours later we were taken to the court room and told that the court had come to a verdict, even without me giving evidence. I wondered why I was not allowed to give evidence, it was all due to my mum, she must have given some evidence against me like saying that I was in no fit state to give any evidence or something like that. Anyway the court had given a verdict, which was he could be bound over to keep the peace for a year, and if not he had to pay a £350 fine. Whatever it was it was not enough, he should have got a sentence, if anything. After the court case, as we came out of the court the barrister who was defending me came over to me and shock me hand saying how brave I am to face everyone like that. I didn't know what to say, so I didn't say anything and just shook his hand and smiled.

After we had been in the court we went into the 'Pizza Hut' for something to eat. That took a couple of hours after we went to the railway station to catch the trains home, one to Addlestone and one to Folkestone. I had the choice, either to go with my mum or to go with my future husband David. Which would you choice? Your right I chose to go with my future husband David. We said that we would see my mum on the Friday 8th February because my brother Stephen is getting married on Saturday 9th February.

On Thursday 7th February we had some snow. I just hope it doesn't stop us from getting up to my brother Stephen's wedding. On Friday 8th February the snow was even thicker than it was the day before. We decided to leave at about 2pm from Folkestone to get to Addlestone because it normally takes about three hours to do the journey. This time it took us about 6 hours, well 8pm that's the time my Uncle Frank picked us up from a station that was covered deep in snow and no one in sight, well that is apart from us. Luckily my Uncle Frank knew what stations are where as he worked for the railway at that particular time.

It was Saturday 9th February and Stephen was getting married to Melanie T this afternoon. My mum had brought a summery dress to wear in all that snow and to top that she was wearing a pair of sandals. I bet she was freezing. The vicar that married Stephen and Melanie T was one of Melanie T's form tutors back in 1984/5; he was also an old geography teacher of mine. The wedding went off fine. We stood out in the snow having our photographs taken. My mum was freezing to death in her brand new summers dress. I was wearing a blue suit I had brought in Woking market and a pair of black boots with a black hat and a black small bag that all matched.

On Wednesday 13th February I had to go up to the Adkinson Morley Hospital for an Angiogram. This is where they put a die in threw the groin ant watch it go around the brain/heart. There is a 5% chance that epilepsy will develop and guess what I took that 5% chance, I developed epilepsy. David came and visited me in hospital while I was in there, which was nice. I had an epileptic fit whilst he was visiting, but that did not put him off me, which I was glad. I was in there for only a few days, and then I was allowed home.

David and I were going to live together but my mum would not let us, she said that the only way we were going to live together is if we were going to get married. So we said fine, and went down to see the vicar at St Paul's Church in Addlestone, Surrey and arrange a date for us to get married. We arranged it to be on Saturday 22nd June 1991. This was only three months away, but that did not worry us. My mum said that she would love to make the wedding dress. So I said ok, but I would choose the pattern. This was alright with my mum. So the following day we went down to buy the material for the dress. It was cotton and all the little bits to go with it as well. Instead of having a bouquet of flowers for me as I suffer with hay fever, my mum was going to make a heart shaped cushion with my name and David's name on it with the date we got married on it. She was also going to make something smaller for the bridesmaids as well.

We had to decide who to choose for our bridesmaids. There were my cousins, Claire and Phillippa, my school friend Caroline G. That was on my side. On David's side there was his niece, Aimee, and Sally (the Down's syndrome girl I mentioned earlier). That left an odd one we decided to ask Margaret, because she had never been married before and it had been her biggest dream to be a bridesmaid, so we asked her, and she said yes. So that made six. We have told all the families concerned except Sally's; that they would have to but their own dresses; we are going around Sally's tomorrow for tea so we will tell her then.

Today we are going to visit Sally and her family; we are not expected there until 5pm so we went around to the park to sit on the bench for a while. When it was time we went round there to their house; they have a lovely looking house from the outside. Inside we went through into the living room throw into the garden where Sally was sitting in a large garden. We went up to Sally and said hello. We started talking, that's when David mentioned about Sally being one of our bridesmaids. Sally said she would love to be one, but she would have to buy her own dress. She asked what colour it would have to be. We said pink.

A couple of months before we get married, David went down to the flats in Hythe, Kent, that were in Sir John Moore Avenue, to set up our things in our new flat. It was a nice flat, it was a purpose built flat for a disabled person, so that everything was a level height for a person in a wheelchair. David had already started to make friends with some of the neighbours; two of they are Judy and Brian King, they were very nice people. I used to call Brian 'my little honey bunch', mind you there were a few people I used to call my little honey bunch.

It came to the night before my wedding day; I am supposed to have my hen night. It was alright I suppose my mum, my Nan Hoy, my sister-in-law Melanie T, Caroline G and Sandra were there. They all had an alcoholic drink except for my mum who was only drinking diet coke and I was drinking pineapple juice. We had a good laugh about one thing and another. The only thing was we all went home by 10 o'clock at night at night. I was soba what a bore.

My wedding day

I got up at my usual time because today was going to be a busy day for everyone. Later on this morning I was going to the hairdressers to get my hair done ready for this afternoon at 4.30pm when I was due to walk down the aisle. It must have been about 2pm when I received a telephone call from Andrew (the boy I met at college), he asked what I was doing, and I replied 'getting ready for my wedding at 4.30pm this afternoon'. And with that he quickly hung up, I don't know why? I think he must have telephoned me to ask me out for a date or something like that. Whatever it was he never asked me.

I had already asked my Uncle Martin if he could drive my dad and me to the church, and he had agreed. He had already dropped my Aunt Brenda and my cousin Phillippa off at the church. My cousin Claire could not make it as she had a 'Brownies/Guides' camp to go to instead. Anyway back to the wedding. My Uncle Martin drove us to the church for 4.30pm. We were a few minutes late but that was expected, seeing that I was in a wheelchair. We made sure all the bridesmaids had their heart shaped cushions and were ready to walk down the aisle. But to everyone's surprise, I walked from the car and down the aisle, but the wheelchair was waiting for me at the altar with a chair next to it for David to sit in. We said our vows, missing out the bit about having children, because I cannot have children; which the vicar knew about.

The wedding went perfectly, except David's real father did not turn up so his Step-father Ron stepped in and signed the wedding certificate along with my dad. David's real father turned up for the reception, a bit late, but as they say 'better late than never'. The wedding ceremony took half an hour, and when that finished I managed to walk out holding on to David's arm. Passing my Nan Norgate (on the way out) she passed me a cheque for £100; she was not talking to my mum at that moment so she did not come to the reception, which was a shame but that was between my mum and my Nan.

The reception went alright to start with. It was held at the local pub (it has been pulled down now and flats been built in its place), The Dukes Head. We were the first ones to arrive there, but were shortly followed by the rest of the guests. As people arrived they put envelopes into the 'Wishing Well' which was by the door. The best man, David's Uncle Roger, made sure that everyone had a drink as it was time to make the speeches, and sure enough Roger did. We gave out our crosses for the bridesmaids and our gift for our best man. We also gave a cross to my third grandmother Margaret; I said I would treat her like a Bridesmaid, and I did! After that the music started and the rain started as well, but never mind it was a reception that you cannot forget!

About an hour through I decided to go home and get changed so Roger took me and Caroline G back to my mum and dad's so that I could get changed. Roger said that he would wait in the car, while Caroline G came inside with me. I changed in to a pair of trousers and a striped shirt. It took me about 15 minutes, after that Roger took us back to the reception.

Our reception was different to normal ones; you see we did not have presents because we had all the essential things' like: towels, tea towel, clocks, knife/forks, sauce pans etc. The only things we really needed were a double bed and a washing machine. So we had a 'Wishing Well', where people put in whatever they want. We got about £700, which was a lot of money in 1991.

As I mentioned before the reception started off fine. I was going round all the guests one at a time, when I got to my second cousin Freddie and his wife Sue. When Freddie offered to buy me a drink, I agreed, and went with him to the bar. I was only drinking pineapple juice. On the way back, I passed my drink down to Sue and went to step down to her level when I stepped down too far and fell back and knocked myself out cold. An ambulance was called. In the ambulance, the ambulance driver had to ask the directions to the hospital. David had to say that he did not know himself because he was new to the area himself.

When we eventually got to the hospital I had come round. The hospital staff had decided to keep me in overnight. David's sister Chris came up the hospital because her youngest daughter Aimee (one of our bridesmaids), wanted to see me, to make sure I was alright. Later that night David slept in the chair next to me in the hospital, so you could say I was the one that said 'not tonight David', because I had the headache.

The next day (Sunday 23rd June 1991) our friend of the family Molly, came with my Dad to pick us up from the hospital and to take us home to Hythe, Kent. My mum could not come with us because she could not fit in Molly's mini. We left after dinner so we got there about 4ish.

David had been to our flat before and set things out, the only thing missing was a double bed but in its place were two single beds. My dad and Molly didn't stay for long because Molly had to be up early next morning as she had to open the paper shop, and my dad had to be up early for his milk round.

A few weeks later my dad, my eldest brother Stephen and his wife Melanie T came down in a van to bring all my belongings (my clothes, my dressing tables, my wardrobe and all my soft toys). They didn't stay to long as my dad had to be up early next morning for his milk round.

In July, August and September 1991 David took driving lessons, and in September he took his driving test and passed. I was well pleased; all he had to do now was to find a car that we could afford. David looked in the papers. And there was one, a ford escort mark 2 for £350; it was a V registration (an old V registration). We went to have a look at it, the spare wheel was the original wheel that had never been used, and the car was in good condition. So we brought it there and then.

We had it for six months before some old women crashed in to us and the car was a right off. Luckily I was not in the car at the moment I was in the hospital. I had asked David to go and get me a McDonalds, so if I hadn't have asked him we might still have that car.

I spent a lot of time in hospital because of my epilepsy, mainly causing problems in the evening or during the night time. Mind you there was one time in December 1991 when I went into hospital for an operation, this was to be sterilised. This time people are supposed to stay in for two days but because of my medical history I was told to stay in for four days at least.

1992

It was at the beginning of 1992 that we had a telephone call from David's real father saying 'Help I am in trouble with the police. Can you come and get me?'

What were we supposed to do but go and get his Father? So we hired a Bluebird car and went up to Oxford. When we got up there his Father was just going to go into court, not for sentencing but just for a hearing. I was told to wait outside because I was in a wheelchair and there were steps leading up to the courtroom. David went ahead because he wanted to see what his Father was being charged for. After the court case had been heard David came back to me.

After the court case had been heard David's Father had been released on bail. So that means that he could come home with us. He was due to be back in court the following week. When he came home with us, David and himself went into Folkestone, Kent to his father's bank and arranged it so that David could withdraw money on his behalf. There was about £20.000 in there. So by the time came home David was an executor for his father.

It had been three days since David's father had been with us when there had been a knock at the door, it was the police. There had been an incident in Folkestone and they pointed the finger straight away at David's father. Just because he was new to the area they automatically thought it was David's father. So they arrested David's father even though we said that he had been with us all the time.

The day of the court case, David's Aunt Jenny came with us because she came with a van to clear out his Father's flat. We went to the court first to hear how long he had got, 6 years. It was not to long because he gave himself up, instead of them finding out. After the court case we went to his flat, the trouble was we didn't have his key so we had to call the police to break into the flat. They came and they made a good job of breaking the door frame, but never mind it's only a policeman doing his job.

Once we got into the flat we took all his belongings down to the van. We decided to take most of the furniture: the wardrobe, the wall units from the front room. We decided to leave the settee, arm chair and fridge, as they were too big. We took all the pictures down off the walls, so he had plenty of pictures.

David's father had so much stuff, almost enough stuff to start again if he wanted too. In the end David and I have said that he could live with us when he comes out of prison, if he wants to.

By this time we had got in touch with mobility about getting a car and they accepted our claim. We chose a red mini metro whose registration number plate was J719 MKL and because it was nice and compact, just what we needed.

It was early January and we had just been up visiting my parents in Addlestone when my epilepsy took hold of me. It was a session of grand mull ones with the arching back. Luckily for David we were just coming past Maidstone, Kent so we went straight into the hospital there. As soon as I was taken in I was taken up to Intensive Care because as soon as I was coming out of one fit I was going back into another. So I don't remember much about the first few days. After that, when I was taken down to the wards, I was taken down to the mixed wards. It was nice, there was this tall male nurse called Steve, he was about 6 foot 6 inches (or there abouts) with blonde hair. If only I was a foot taller and single (dreams dreams).

Now this mixed ward (I liked it) I made friends with this male patient next to me. He was in because he had a heart attack when he was driving his lorry. I liked to watch his heart monitor as it went across each time, and he used to watch out for me each time I used to have a fit.

While I was in Maidstone I had an appointment to see a consultant in the William Harvey Hospital, Ashford, Kent which was just down the road from Maidstone. So as not to make things complicated Maidstone arranged for an ambulance to take me to the William Harvey Hospital. On the trip between the two hospitals I had 7 fits. The ambulance crew and a nurse (a temp nurse) wheeled me in to see the consultant while I was having a fit. So what does the consultant do but have a go at the ambulance crew for bringing me, then has a go at the nurse for not being the proper nurse. Then turns to me and starts tapping me on the head. David says that you've only got to tap me on the forehead like that to knock me out cold, so what does the consultant continues to do but tap me on the head and I am out cold.

After the ambulance crew and nurse had come out of there, they all said that they would put that in a report about the consultant and that they hope that David would too. Later that day, a consultant from the Maidstone Hospital came to see us. He had heard about what had happened with the other consultant in the William Harvey Hospital and wanted to offer his services, we accepted.

I had some really bad news while I was in Maidstone Hospital. It was that my third Grand Mother Margaret had died. It is a shame but I look at it like this at least we filled her biggest dream of becoming a bridesmaid. My mum came down for Margaret's funeral; it was held in the church in Folkestone, none of her family arranged her funeral David's Aunt Jenny did it all as at the time she was living at her home.

David gave me a surprise, he wrote off to Des O'Conner to get a signed autograph for me. Wasn't that nice of him? I still have that autograph but the writing has faded, I would love to get another one someday but who knows when?

A few months later, our friend Liz came down to stay with us for a short stay. I met her when she went to the Queen Elizabeth Training College in Leatherhead, Surrey and she was friends with David. I liked her but I didn't like her, if you know what I mean. She also suffers from epilepsy but hers' are a different level to mine.

When she stayed with us for a short time, this time my epilepsy was at its worst. There was one evening about 10 pm; I awoke David not in bed beside me but to find him in the living room with Liz lying on the put-you-up bed top less and David massaging her. I walked in straight passed them not looking at them, walked straight over to the fridge to get a glass of orange juice, I then turned and walked out of the living room back into the bed room not looking at what they were doing. David got up and followed me into the bed room mumbling something; I was not listening to what he was saying; so I just said 'ok darling, I want to go to sleep now'. So he went back to the living room to clear his things away. I never did find out what he did say that night.

A couple of mornings later I was having a lazy morning in bed, when David and Liz decided to come and join me. David and I had talked about having a three some in bed, but I mean I never dreamed it would be anything like this, but I can say I have done it now. We only did it the once, I think we were a disappointment for Liz, we were not up to her standard. I was only a beginner at the sort of thing, I mean what does she expect, it to be handed to her on a gold plate.

My epilepsy was still playing up as much as last year, but that did not stop me from joining a disabled swimming club once a week. They taught me to swim using an arm band on my right arm and just using my left arm and my left leg. I can swim better than David can and he swims normally, now that's saying something!! We do this once a week. For instance, one week in Folkestone swimming pool I swam their main pool 15 times while David only managed to swim it 6 times.

The swimming club committee had their annual meeting and once a year chose a couple to go away on holiday to Great Yarmouth, and they chose David and me. What a surprize!! The reason why they decided to pick us is because we never had a honeymoon, so this was a late honeymoon. And we enjoyed ourselves especially when I entered David for the Knobbly Knees contest and he got his own back when he entered me for the judges. Even on this holiday my epilepsy comes with me, but David managed to cope with it by himself.

While we were in Great Yarmouth we got some of those naughty stickers you put on the back window of the car. One of the said 'Me not silly, me wear condom on my Willy'. Now that is not too bad, is it? Well there were some of the residents around Sir John Moore Avenue that could not take a joke, so they got in contact with the local councillor, who got in contact with us. David said if they don't like it they can talk to us nicely instead of sending rude comments across the path. A couple of days later David was out and there was a phone call, I took it. It was this councillor and he said I see you have not removed the stickers yet? And I said 'the car is in my name and as far as I am concerned the stickers are staying', and with that hung up. After that I was shaking, after all it is not every day I say things like that to a councillor. And after that we did not hear any more from the councillor or the old ladies.

In the summer we had one of David's nieces' staying with us. We had been swimming in Folkestone and were on our way back to our flat, when a Brigadier pulled out of the council offices in Hythe, Kent and smacked straight into the side of us. It frightened our niece but apart from that she was alright. Me, it made me bang my head against the side of my door and made me have a terrific epileptic fits. The police were called and they got rid of the Brigadier before they called for the doctor to see to me. As they watched the Brigadier back they had to bang on the back of his car because he backed into the side of the police car, but they still let him go.

Doctor Foster (our doctor at that particular time) came along as it was only across the road from the surgery. He gave me some injections but they did not seem to work so he suggested calling for an ambulance. The ambulance took about 15 minutes to arrive. By this time the Brigadier was well out of sight.

When the ambulance arrived at the hospital I was just coming round. My husband, who was David, came round the curtain, I did not recognize him, and I did not know who anyone was, not even my mum or my dad.

The hospital even released me even though I did not know who I was or where I was going. David assured them and me that I was in safe hands. When we got to what we called home David telephoned my mum and told her what happened. Between the two of them they arranged a meeting for the Sunday (today being Wednesday).

On Sunday my mum, my dad, my brother Kevin and my school friend Caroline G (also one of my brides' maids) came down to visit me. They came down ready to jog my memory, but they did not succeed, not even a little bit. But what I have told you so far is what they have told me. But don't worry I do get some of my memory back; otherwise I would not have been able to write this book.

One thing I do remember is that David's two cousins, Darren and Kevin, used to come down to our flat in Sir John Moore Avenue, Hythe, Kent. We used to go down to our local pub in the evenings. I can remember one particular time we all had our usual non-alcoholic larger and non-alcoholic wine for me. Anyway, we were all walking back, when I couldn't walk anymore. So David and his cousins decided to carry me. If anyone had watched us they would have died laughing because it was a sight for sore eyes.

My epilepsy was being a real pain this year, for instance, it was a very wet late last night when my epilepsy started up. I had grand mall session; I was fitting like a trouper. The ambulance came to our flat at Sir John Moore Avenue, instead of parking in the car park the ambulance came right up on the path and spoiled some of the plants. Some of the neighbours' complained about it, don't worry about me just worry about some stupid plants which can be replaced.

It was November and I was in Buckland Hospital in Dover following a spell of epileptic fits. The cubical I was in was diabolical, there was blood stains on the curtains and up the walls, in the locker there was a mouldy orange and a full bottle of laxative tablets. It was discussing, you would have thought there would have been a cleaner to clean these things but there was not there was only cleaners' to clean the floors.

While I was in there I counted how many tablets I had to take a day, 24 in all. No wonder I was more like a zombie not knowing what day was which.

I came out of hospital on the Wednesday and on the Friday I said to myself right I am not going to take anymore tablets, and put them on one side and did not touch them anymore. And do you know I have felt 100% better since.

1993

Meanwhile, David was having a spending spree with his Father's money. Who had control of because his Father had signed all his money over to him while he was in prison. It was as if it was like his Father owed him the money from all the years he did not know him. We did visit him when he sent a 'Visiting Order' to see him all the way up in Oxford, that was until he was moved down to Devon, which is a long way for us to visit, but we managed to visit a few times.

I am still off my tablets and it is coming up to my 21st birthday and I am having a birthday party. David asked the hospital if they could do the food for my party and they replied yes. The food was wonderful there was enough there to feed an army. The birthday cake was lovely. It was chocolate sponge with white icing and a picture of a young lady on the front of it.

We had invited my mum, dad and my younger brother Kevin. We also invited Caroline G (one of my brides' maids), the members of my swimming group, and some members of David's family. I totally enjoyed myself. My mum felt a bit left out, so David gave her the job of cutting the cake up. That kept her quiet, and made her felt useful. The music which was hired was a duet. We held a raffle and raffled off some large soft toys, my mum got a soft dog and there were four other prizes to go. We raised something like £45 in all, which was not bad. At the end of the evening there was so much food left over that everyone took a dish full home.

A fortnight later we were moving home in to a flat on the sea front, Pensand House, South Road, Hythe, Kent. David's brother already lives in the flat opposite but one. He lives there with his common-law wife, and once a fortnight he has one of his sons' come over to stay for the weekend.

Once a week David used to go to the Victoria Hospital, Folkestone to do an hour of fitness with Jack Bryan, I used to go and read a book or to watch David or watch the other men, I am not sure which!!!

One Wednesday I stayed at home and David brought one of the other men home with him, his name was Steve and he was about 6 foot tall with brown hair with grey bits in it. That was due to old age, he was 45. We both said to him that he could come up any time he wanted to because we would be in any time. He said thank you and he would accept our offer.

David got himself a voluntary job in driving, sometime he would be out from 9.30am in the morning until 4pm in the afternoon. I would not mind but it left me all alone with no-one to talk to, nothing to do after I had done the house work, that is until Steve came to play!!

We had been in our flat for four months when we had decided to have foreign students (French) for the summer period. We had our first student, it was a fine young man, and his name was Sabastein. He was 15 years old soon to be 16, if I remember rightly it was his birthday while he was over here.

It started off on this summers' day (while this French student was here) when David had gone out early and would be out until about 5pm that evening. I had done all the hovering and dusting, made our bed, made the student's bed and tided the kitchen, actually done everything. It was about 12 noon and there was a knock at the door, I answered it, it was Steve. He came in. We had a sandwich and a chat in the front room. Then it started, Steve said something and I replied and he came over to where I was sitting and we started kissing. Then we started, Steve pulled his shorts' down and me pulled my skirt up and my knickers' down. Then he stuck his penis inside me, it felt so good. In and out, the feeling, now I know what the feeling of a real man feels like. Steve would not come inside me, I don't know why; perhaps it was something he just did not want to do or something like that.

Another time we were on the way to Canterbury, Kent when we stopped in a field. Steve got a blanket out of the car and laid it out on the ground, we got on top. On top of the blanket we made love, he ended up with no clothes on and I ended up with nothing on top and my skirt pushed up around my middle but nothing else on. We ended up kissing and doing David's favourite number, number 69, in case you don't know what one of these is I will tell you. A 69 is where a man and a woman go head and foot, then the man and woman lick or suck the private parts.

Another time was in Folkestone, Kent we were up at the Leas. I was wearing a skirt with no knickers' and a t-shirt, and we were walking along the Leas when we came along a bench, were we sat down, me on top of him and started kissing and cuddling. We did this for about half an hour, then I stopped because I noticed a couple who had been sitting on the bench next to us had been giving us dirty looks. So we stopped and got up and walked off towards Steve's car. When we got there we drove off up to Steve's home because his wife had heard so much about me that she wanted to meet me. I felt so guilty about meeting her and having this affair with her husband, it just did not fill right, and then there were their two children. I do feel so guilty!!!

One morning David went out and Steve phoned me and said it's no good he has to be with me for ever. I was shocked, I had no idea it would be like this, but I agreed to be with him.

I waited for David to come back and the way I acted by not letting him kiss me or cuddle me he knew something was wrong. He asked and asked and finally I told him. He took my keys off me so I could not unlock the front door. He went out of the front door and locked it after him. He went next door to get his brother who came in and called me all the names under the sun. Meanwhile, Steve had turned up down below and I was shouting to him from the flat bedroom window.

David had called a police officer to come because he did not want me to go, but the way I was feeling I wanted to go. The police officer let me go, and Steve welcomed me with open arms.

We went to Steve's home, little did we know that David had already phoned up there to let Steve's wife know what had happened. Once we got there Steve went in first and I heard all the names under the sun insinuated at me, so I turned round and headed for the car. About ten minutes later Steve came out with a bag of clothes. We made our way towards Maidstone, we were going to go up to Steve' parents place, where ever that is.

We stopped half way at the car park, where Steve got out of the car so I got out of the car too. We saw this other fellow so Steve started to follow him, holding my hand I followed behind. We saw that this man climbed over this tree that had fallen across a path way covering a little pocket, so that nobody could see in unless you knew you were there. Anyway, the three of us were in this pocket and I was the only female in there and there were two males, you can guess what was going to happened, can't you? I didn't have much choice in the matter, I couldn't really say no, could I? At least I did not let either of them come inside of me, I was too proud to let them try, after all I was David's and I had married him.

When we got to Maidstone we stopped the car, we both had a thought and a chat, and come to the conclusion that we should go back home. There was a phone box across the road and we went across there to phone our partners to ask for forgiveness. We tried David first there was no answer, so we tried his mum's she said go to her place. Now it was time to try his wife. I did try to apologise but she just gave me a load of verbal abuse back which I could not blame her. So I just gave the phone back to Steve, and went back to the car, he followed in about 5-10 minutes later.

Steve drove me to David mum's home in Lydd, Kent. When we got there he got my bag out of the boot of his car, and while he gave it to me he said how sorry he was and he hoped that we could still be friends. I said that maybe we could, but in the back of my mind there was a bit of hate building up. He also said that he had organised a sponsored run around the Radner Park, Folkestone, Kent on their Donkey Derby Day and perhaps we could go down there. I said maybe.

Inside Joan Allen's (David's mum) place we sat in the kitchen and talked, well I mainly listened to what she had to say. Then she asked why I did it? And I answered that I did it because David had left me alone for hours and hours, and I just wanted company, Joan said she could see it from both points of view, but wait for David to come and the two of us have a chat and see where things go from there.

About an hour later David turned up in our car with his brother and his common-law wife. His brother and common-law wife were there to do some odd jobs around their Nan's house which was two doors away from their mum's house. Meanwhile, David and I went for a walk to talk things through. We must have walked for about an hour or so, we both did some talking. David said sorry for not being there when he was needed and I said that was alright, I could have gone around David's brothers' if I got lonely because his common-law wife is always in. In fact that is what I will do in future.

After we had finished our talk we had decided to try again. On the way home David's brother and his other half never said a word to me, come to think of it they never said a word to David either, I wonder why!

The next morning I woke up with the sound of the sea lapping up against the beach, it was so beautiful. I soon got up. David was in the kitchen making breakfast. He had already made the student's and sent him on his way out with his school for the day. He asked what shall we do today, I replied what about going to the Donkey Derby, because I knew that Steve was doing a sponsored run around Radner Park, Folkestone. David face lightened up as if he was up to mischief, but what could he do.

When we got to Radner Park it was packed with people, of all shapes and sizes. In the middle of the green was the donkeys all lined up ready for the derby. There was a man taking money for the bets. And on the outskirts, was the lads, running for the sponsors. On one corner was Steve, we never went over to him, instead we stood on the opposite corner. We only stayed there for about half an hour then we left.

After that we heard nothing from Steve or any of his family. That did not bother me and I know that it certainly did not bother David.

Later in the year we went to pick up Liz from the YMCA, because she was staying in one of their apartments. Liz came down to stay for a week or so. We were doing fine until she did something that did not agree with the both of us, so we told Liz she had to go. She said she would go by bus, so she had to walk across the green before she came to the main road, whatever way she went we could see her from our window.

We waited and waited but no Liz was sighted. We waited for 40 minutes but still no sight of her, but by this time there was a knock at the door. It was Liz being helped up by a middle aged man, who said that she was found having a fit down by the road side. That is why we could not see her, because she was having a fit by the road, typical. David helped her in, he said that this still does not change things she still going back but this time he was driving her back there himself. And he did!

Our friend Victor and his partner Raymond had just lost their dog, they had to have him put down due to old age. So they have just got themselves a Jack Russell and named her Tammy. They brought her up to our flat and she is so sweet. I wish they would stay that sweet all the time, but they all grow up sooner or later.

Living in this flat is like living in a draft box, every time we had wind the carpets waved with the wind. We had to keep the plugs in the plug holes because we got drafts through them. When we sat on the toilet seat you rocked from side to side. The frame on the bedroom door came out because it was not screwed to the walls. The cupboard in the kitchen was not fixed to the walls so when you went to put things in to it, it came away from the wall. And finally there was a hole in the floor in the corner of the floor in the spare room.

The only things of these that were sorted out were the frame on the door, and the cupboard in the kitchen. The rest were still waiting to be done when we left. It was like next door in David's brothers' place it was just the same. His carpets are the same as ours; the plugs are just the same. Now have you ever heard of opening windows by taking the whole window out, window frame and all, well they did!

One morning David woke up and stretched, like anyone would. This morning he woke with a terrible pain in his neck, he just put it down to the way he slept. As the day went on the pain got worse and worse, so David suggested that he would go down to the local hospital to get it checked out, I said I would go with him but I would watch a television programme first, because I must watch my Prisoner Cell Block H. That was when it was on. When we got down to the hospital they said David had to wear a collar because he had sprained his neck, but to make sure he was to come back to Fracture Clinic on Wednesday (I think that's when it was) and see what they say.

On Wednesday David went to the Fracture Clinic, like they said in the A&E the other day. In the Fracture Clinic they x-rayed David's neck and it showed a fracture mark across his neck. He had actually broken his neck, yet things he has done throughout his life and yet he has broken his neck. No wonder the poor thing was in so much pain. The hospital gave him another collar and some strong painkillers and they said they would send a letter to our doctor.

1994

In the spring of this year I started at college in Folkestone, Kent. I started doing a NVQ Office Practice course level 1, it was supposed to be a 6 week course, but because I was the only disabled person on the course I was allowed to do the next 6 week course, so in fact I did 12 weeks instead. And because I was doing 12 weeks I was allowed to do parts of NVQ Office Practice course level 2. I only did 2 parts of level 2, and they were Finance and Word Processing. If I wanted to do the rest of level 2 I would have to go to Dover College and study there. But I did not fancy travelling all the way to there and I did not fancy all the things that it involved studying such as French.

While I was at college we had to move home's, from Pensand House, Hythe to Elm Road, St Mary's Bay. On our way to Elm Road we had to sell all of our furniture because we were going from an unfurnished place into a furnished place, it was a shame because we had some beautiful pieces of furniture, but they had to go.

David picked me up from college that afternoon after he had taken our bits and pieces to Elm Road. We were glad to leave Pensand House with all its faults but it had a beautiful view overlooking the sea. But I am looking forward to living in a bungalow that does not have any faults at all, welcome Elm Road.

This year we had our red mini metro stolen from the car park opposite the police station in Ashford, Kent. We were in the bingo hall playing bingo, we didn't win. Anyway, we were in there playing bingo, after we had finished we went out to the car park, to the disabled parking space and it was empty. Our car, it was gone. Where could it be? We went to the police station and told them exactly what had happened. When David told the officer on duty where we lived, St Mary's Bay, the officer said 'Where's that?' I mean it is supposed to be on part of their mapping area and they ask where it is. I don't know what is the world coming to?

We ended up phoning David's step-father Ron up to come and get us, because David did ask if a police car could take me home, it did not matter about himself he could walk home but I phoned Ron. He took us home, I was a bit annoyed because I had a white stick in the front of the car and this meant I had to send off for a new one.

We had no news about the car, I expect it is probably out of the country by now. In a way we were glad that the car was stolen because of the mileage we would have had to pay on it, because it was a Motability car and the mileage would have cost us at least £700 and we could not afford that. We had to contact Motability about the car being stolen and getting a new one, we would have to wait six months for a new one to come through. Six months, I can't wait that long. David had an idea to phone on the radio and see whether they could help, and sure enough they did. This couple were listening to David's plea on the radio and had the mini sitting there doing nothing. So they offered it to David free of charge, and he said yes. So we were getting a mini, until they want it back, which could be about four to five months, which will suit us, fine.

David's mum, Joan had recently got a new dog, a small dog. I fell in love with her as soon as I saw her and I think she liked me too.

When I first saw Mitsy (that is her name) I picked her up and she fitted in to the palm of my hand, now that is small.

Joan let Mitsy come away to our bungalow for a holiday. We loved to have her. By the time she came to us she was a lot bigger than she was before. She loved her time in the mini because she climbed up on to the back against the window and went to sleep.

Our time David had a restless night, he took an over dose of tablets because his neck was giving him a lot of pain. Anyway, David and Mitsy went in the mini at 1am in the morning and drove all the way to Tesco's in Folkestone, Kent to get some cigarettes (which he didn't smoke), but Mitsy was there. So there was David and Mitsy out shopping, and there was I at home worried because of David taking all these tablets. About 4am David came in with Mitsy behind him. Mitsy did alright because she got some hearts and I got some trousers and socks. In future I am going to keep David's keys hidden at night so that he cannot do it again.

1995

It is time to change our car. The next car we are going to get is a white Corsa M582 OKM. We decided to get this car because this car was more spacious than the car we had before. And that it is what I wanted in a car, space and height. A car must have height because since the car accident, I must have a car that has some height above the opposite cars headlights because I cannot have their lights blearing at me so I cannot see. I really hate that, don't you?

There was one time my Nan Hoy was having problems with my Uncle Frank, I don't know exactly what the problem was; all I know was my Nan was upset. We went all the way up to Bagshot to take my Nan shopping, we didn't mind but my mum lives about 25 minutes down the road from her, now why couldn't she have taken her?

So my Nan Hoy wanted a holiday, time to get away from my Uncle Frank, so we suggested that she came down to stay with us for a while; and she agreed. So she and her friend Karen (a young woman in her 20ist) came down; Karen came down for one week while my Nan came down for two. They had a wonderful time down here. Karen pushed my Nan about in her wheelchair, whilst I had an appointment up at the William Harvey Hospital, a check-up and David was doing his voluntary driving, like usual.

It was a frosty morning David and I were playing in the kitchen and I attempted to run with David following behind. When suddenly I tripped and fell banging my head on the way down on the unit in front of me and knocking myself out cold. Of course that made David call for an ambulance and within five minutes an ambulance was there. David explained what had happened and explained my medical history, about my stroke (my CVA when I was 16).

The ambulance men took me in the ambulance to the William Harvey Hospital. Meanwhile David was following behind in the car. When we got to the hospital I was just about coming around. They kept me in for 24 hours just to make sure I was alright. I was alright after that; I must stop that game of cat and mouse with David because the mouse keeps on getting injured (trust me).

Another time I had a really bad migraine, I suffer from these at least one a week. Anyway, this particular time David was out at bingo so he was not due in until 9.30pm, and this migraine was getting worse and worse. When David came in he found me banging my head against the furniture, crying; holding my head saying to myself 'go away'. So he phoned the doctor up on the emergency line at Lydd, Kent and the doctor said 'bring her over to the ambulance station'. So David made sure that I was ready to go outside; then he took me outside in the car to the ambulance station. Once we got there, he struggled to get me out of the car and in to the ambulance station. Inside there we saw the doctor for a few minutes and he gave me a letter to give in at the A&E at the hospital when we got there. So we had to make our own way there, they were too busy watching football on television.

1996

It was in this year when my dad had to go up to Scotland to get my Nan Norgate's body because she died whilst on holiday with my Great Auntie Emmie. They had gone up there for their Christmas holiday but my Nan had never finished it. What a shame!

I think me Nan must have known that this was her last year because she had brought everyone a Christmas present, which she had not done for the past five years since she had fallen out with my mum.

It was a sunny day for her funeral, which had been unusual for that time of year (January). My Uncle Martin, Aunt Brenda and cousin, Claire came up from Henfield, whereas we came up from St Mary's Bay to Addlestone, Surrey, which was where she was living.

Throughout the year we were busy with French students. From March until about the middle of the year we got them for two to four nights, but the middle months we got one student for three weeks at a time, which we preferred. We have been doing this for a few years now and we have always have been getting on with the children. I suppose it is because we treat the children as though they were our own and that is what the children like.

We went away for Christmas this year; we went all the way to France. One of our French students' invited us to come for Boxing Day. We left on Christmas Day at about 5pm, the last boat out. We travelled all night, as far as we could possible go, then I fell asleep.

David drove until he couldn't see anything. There was nothing but empty fields everywhere. Then he went to sleep himself. When we both woke up the whole ground was white with snow, we could not believe our eyes.

With the ground all white with snow it was almost impossible to see which way we had been before, but we somehow managed to find a way out of this sheet of whiteness. We came to a garage that was open so we stopped to get some petrol as we were getting short of it. David asked someone there if they knew the way to where we were going. That was when this kind person not only showed us the way on the map but they took us to the front door of the student. Wasn't that kind of that person?

We arrived at our students' just as they were finishing dining. They introduced themselves; there was Mireille (our French student), the mother, the father, the sister and the grandmother (the mother of the father of Mireille). They did offer us something to eat but we both said no thank you, but we would like to rest for a little while as we have been travelling all night, so they showed us the bedroom we were going to sleep in during our stay there.

During our stay there we were shown some interesting things. We were shown some caves where mushrooms were grown. The caves went on for miles, and so did the mushrooms, they grow in all different colours, shapes and sizes. The colours include yellow, red and white. Personally I don't like them myself, but David does and so does the French family, so we brought some for dinner that day or the following day.

The family are wine producers; they produce red, white and champagne wine. All the wines taste very nice. The mother was telling us that once the grapes are all picked all the workers get together and have a festival (like what we call a harvest festival).

While we stayed with Mireille we also visited our other student. We were invited around to her house for dinner, Mireille came too because none of our other students' family could speak English so Mireille was our translator. When we all sat down to dinner, we started off with a soup. When we had finished the soup I said to David how nice it was and that it tasted like sardines. David asked what kind of soup it was, and he found out it was lobster soup. Thank god the family couldn't understand English.

When we left their place in France we took two cases of each of their wines, and it didn't cost much money either. Although it was still snowing the roads were still clear because the French are more equipped when it comes to clearing roads. It was like on the main roads from Paris to Calais the road sweepers were three a breast. Now here in England you would be lucky if you would see one road sweeper let alone three. And the roads are in utter chaos with one bit snow, but I hate to imagine what they are like in a blizzard.

It was December when we heard from the council, they have given us a fortnight to move into an unfurnished bungalow out of a furnished bungalow. This unfurnished bungalow was really nice; it was a two bedroomed place. It had a large sitting room, a small kitchen of that, back of the sitting room was a hall way, off the hall way was a bath room, the spare room and the main bed room. The spare room is big enough to put two signal beds side by side and a signal bedside cabinet in between them. The only trouble is getting furniture for this lovely bungalow which is in New Bridge Way, St Mary's Bay.

Luckily for us the manager who looks after the bungalow we are living in a the moment has told us that he has a property that has some furniture in it that we can offer him a price for it and we can have the furniture. We went up and had a look at the furniture. The furniture was really good; it was army issue furniture so it will last for ever. The furniture we got is: 5 small bedside cabinets, 2 sets of draws, 1 side cabinet for the front room and 1 coffee table. I cannot remember exactly how much we offered the manager but I know it was not less than £100 and he accepted it.

1997

Before we put all the furniture in its right place we had to go out and buy the carpets along with the beds, cooker and the washing machine. And before we laid the carpets we had to do the painting, the front room was a horrible orangey colour; it was so disgusting it would have made you feel sick if you stayed in the same room as it for so long. The carpet which we had chosen for the living room was red, the one which we had chosen for our bed room was a grey and the spare room, well the carpet that was left behind was alright, so we left that as it was.

The kitchen, now that was a different story. The sink was alright, the cooker was fine and the washing machine was fitted alright it was just the unit on top off the machine that just needed replacing. Now the rest of the kitchen needed redoing and re-decorating. Let me tell you about one of cupboard's that had the electric and the gas meter and the fuse box. You had the gas meter sitting on top off the electric meter and the fuse box on top of that and guess what we had a gas leak. And the gas people told us to turn the gas and electric meters off. We told them where they can go. So when they came to fix the leak we asked them to put the both meters outside.

After we got everything settled in our new bungalow we decided we needed a holiday, we decided that we would go and see Mireille in France again. We thought we have been there once so we know the way so we won't get lost. So what do we do but get lost going around the auto-route (like the M25) round Paris, so we pulled over and two police men on motorbikes pulled over. David showed them where we want to go on the map, and the two officers kindly said follow them and they will show us where to go off at the correct junction. Now who said that the French were not nice people, we have been over here twice and both times they have helped us out by going out of their way, now that's what I call kindness.

We spent two holidays over in France this year, because Mireille's family said to us to go over there whenever we wish because their home is always open; that was nice off them. We liked our trips over to see them all, in all our trips over to see them we always took them presents. For instance we took the father a box of cigars, because we knew he enjoys a good smoke after lunch and dinner. Another time we took the family some English made wine, for them to try.

This winter I fell ill with my epilepsy, this time it affected my right ankle and right arm/wrist. My ankle took the worst of it, it went right under, but luckily the centre at the William Harvey Hospital, Ashford, had a splint for that sort of thing. The splint for the ankle went up both sides of the leg, it may look funny but it works. Now the arm/wrist, they had splints for wrists but none suitable for what was needed for me, so they had to make one. The physiotherapist that did the splint for my arm/wrist was ever so nice, he was ever so gentle. I had to see him three times because it took time to fit the splint into shape, but he finally fitted it.

1998

The next car we got was a green Astra R61 YKN. We decided to get this car because there was more room in the back of this car that the Corsa and there was more leg room in the front of the car.

It must have been early January when David had gone round the village hall with his mum, Joan Allen, to play bingo. I was waiting in doors for David to come home about 4ish but he came in at about 3.30ish, I was a bit puzzled. Then David said that his mum has been rushed to hospital because she has had a heart attack in our car while sitting next to him. I wondered why he looked so pale in the face, now I know why.

We then went over to Ron's (David's step-father) and his mum's house, also where David's Nan was. David told Ron what exactly happened, and Ron said he would get up the hospital once he has sorted Nan out. We left Ron's and went straight up the hospital, and were met by one of David's sisters, his sister Chris.

Joan was in intensive care for about five days; then she was taken on to the wards. She was on the ward for a couple of weeks before she was taken to St Thomas' Hospital in London for a triple bye pass. That went alright, all but one of the metal stents took; but that did not matter.

It brought the whole family closer together, that included David's brothers' Stephen and Peter. It also brought David's sister from

Manchester, Sue down. Chris came down from Harlow in Essex and stayed closer by just in case anything happened to her mum.

When Joan was up in St Thomas' we visited her every day, while Chris stayed in the staff quarters because there are some rooms up there for parents or partners to sleep. Joan was getting better all the time she was up there in London. She had improved so much that they said that she could go back to the William Harvey Hospital in Ashford, Kent.

Joan left St Thomas' in good time. She arrived at the William Harvey Hospital at about 3pm'ish. Joan was a diabetic so she needed her insulin an hour before she had anything to eat, but the nurse said they did not have anything on paper so they could not give anything to her. We, the family, all say that it should have been written down on paper from hospital to hospital what medication each patient is on, but for some reason it isn't, or wasn't this time.

It was at one o'clock in the morning when Joan was given her insulin. Chris, David and I were totally discussed at this, but there is nothing that we could do about it. Over the following day Joan was feeling colder than usual, she had six blankets on her and she was still feeling cold. In the evening she went to the toilet, she was told she must have a nurse with her when she goes to the toilet, she had no body. While in the toilet, she was sick, she cleared it up herself. She must have had a fall while she was in there because she had a bruise on her leg.

When she got back to her bed she told a nurse that she had been sick; so the nurse gave her a bowl and told her to get on with it. If I had been there I would have given the nurse a piece of my mind. As it was later that night Joan was rushed back down to intensive care, where as if it didn't help, in the bed next to her was her sister.

She was in there suffering with the same thing as Joan was. She was waiting to go up to London to have the same thing as Joan has done.

When Joan was ready to come out of intensive care Chris made sure that she did not go back on to that ward that she was on before, instead she went on to Kings ward because they seemed a nice ward. Joan was on a side ward because she had so many visitors, cards and gifts.

I used to sit with Joan after I had been to my physiotherapy session downstairs in the centre below once a week. Joan used to tell me when her son Peter came up, that she used to really hate it because she could never tell which mood he used to be in. It was like one time when Joan was in London, Peter went on a two mile round trip just to get a can of larger/fosters. I mean if you cannot go to see someone without having a can of drink then there is something wrong with you.

It was a sad day when Joan died. David and I went in to see her; she just looked as though she was asleep. I couldn't help myself but cry it was as though I was losing a friend, let alone a mother-in-law. Chris felt so guilty because that morning she had her first lay in for a long time, and her mum happened to die on that morning.

The funeral was a sad occasion, David, Peter and Stephen helped to carry Joan's coffin down in to the church and out again. They all had tears in their eyes. I know I cried a lot when she was put in to the Hurst to take her to the crematorium. At the crematorium David and his brothers went to carry the coffin but the ushers said it would be too much for them, so they just walked behind instead.

This year after we had laid Joan, we made friends with two elderly sisters, May and Agnes. They wanted to go on holiday, so we said we would take them. We ended up going to Devon. The rooms that we were supposed to have only had a bath in it, we asked for a shower because three of us can get down in to the bath but cannot get out of it again. So instead of having two rooms they gave us a caravan which had a shower in it, which suited us better.

David had problems while driving down to Devon, he had shingles. It was his first time and only time, we hope. He had it around his right hip, around where his seatbelt goes. So he had to use my sanitary towels for protection against his seatbelt rubbing his side.

The first morning David went to the chemist to see whether he could get some padding for his waist for his shingles. They didn't so he carried on using my sanitary towels instead. It was lucky I brought extra towels with me because David seemed to be using them more than me.

We went to bingo each night on the camp site, but we didn't seem to win a sausage but we enjoyed ourselves. The sisters did win once or twice. The two sisters we went with moaned about everything and moaned about each other.

When we got home the two sisters asked David if he would do a few odd jobs about the home for them. David said that he would. The odd jobs involved: tiling the bathroom, putting a new window in, and painting the outside of the bungalow, painting the wall, building the footpath out the back. These are just a few of the things which David did for the two sisters, and one day David over heard one of the sisters saying to someone 'nobody ever does anything for us'. Well you can imagine how David felt. Well he soon stopped going round there and doing odd jobs for the sisters.

It was also in this year when we took over the bingo from the old gentleman that ran it before us because he was retiring. We brought a new bingo machine, one that showed the numbers that were being called clearly so that everyone could see them.

We started a Christmas raffle with over twenty five prizes, ranging from packets of sweets up to hampers of goodies. We didn't sell as many raffle tickets as we thought we would but you learn from your mistakes.

This December David met Ian Morrison who was the instructor for the martial arts group Taek-won-do. David only joined me up to do this Taek-won-do. Yes I do this Taek-won-do. So we went along on a Wednesday evening and I joined in. I spent most of the time on the floor and everyone was helping me up, but I enjoyed myself. I was the only disabled person there and while I was learning of Ian, Ian was learning of me because Ian had never taught a disabled person before.

1999

The Taek-won-do was going fine. In January I was due to take my first grade-in for Taek-won-do for yellow belt. It was held on one of his Sunday sessions when I couldn't make the morning group because we had our bingo instead. In the afternoon we had a quick dash in to Ashford, Kent to the Taek-won-do for my grade-in. I made it just in time. Whereas all the others had time to practice, I didn't but I had to go straight in to the grade-in.

I failed the patterns but I managed to do all the rest of the things like punches, kicks, defences etc. After the others had done their grade-in's we went upstairs and sat down, where Ian gave his verdict. He passed everyone; that includes me, their belt. I was over the moon. The first person I telephoned was my mum. And all she could say was not congratulations but they took your disabilities in to consideration. I went from feeling over the moon down to feeling so low. How could anyone say something like that, especially a mother to a child?

One incident that happened in Taek-won-do, it was no bodies fault, but when I was sparring with one of the instructor's (Ron a black belt) we both kicked at the same time, our feet entangled and I fell back, banged my head on the floor on the way down. This caused a little fit and about 15 minutes later I came round and I sat up and was ready to start again, but they would not let me. The instructor Ron; said about bringing a helmet in for me to wear to protect my head. So from that day onwards I wore a helmet to protect my head.

Later on in the year I passed another grade-in for Taek-won-do, so that makes me yellow belt green tab, this time I knew better than to tell my mum that I had passed another grade-in. The only thing that bothers me is learning the different language. I mean I found it difficult learning French when I was at school, so I don't know how I am going to get on with this.

With the bingo, we are still doing well. We do one money game and the rest grocery games. Some people have asked David if we could make it an all money game. David said he would look in to it. So David went to see the committee (who did a full money session once a month) and the gambling committee. The gambling committee sent a leaflet back and David read it. You wouldn't believe it even the committee were doing it illegally. So they had to change their bingo or stop it. They soon changed it, not only theirs; they also took over our bingo so that was the end of our bingo. It just was not fair the way they did it. David stayed around for the first Saturday that was supposed to change but there was no bingo because the committee expected David to get all the money in and split it between the two of us, them and us. But we were not having it that way, we decided they can do it all themselves, if they want to! Little did we know it would make a great success of it.

2000

This year I started playing darts. I started playing for the British Legion for the women team, the captain is Diane Tucker. Diane lives just round the corner; she was a new mother to me and David and her husband Brian is like a new father to me. In darts I was rubbish to start with and to prove it the team got the 'wooden spoon', a trophy the losers all get. It proves that we got somewhere in darts, even if it is last place.

At darts I started playing for the British Legion in Dymchurch, Kent. There was one person that was a member of the British Legion that I really hated, and that person I did not wish to see again in my whole live. It was HIM, Richard, that person that assaulted me back in 1988 and 1990. He lived here in Dymchurch and drank in the British Legion. I hated playing darts at the British Legion because he was always there, I could feel his eyes staring at me, even though I was not looking at him. David had told my darts team all about what he had done, so they knew it was best to keep out of his way.

Doing this Taek-won-do has given me enough courage to face this Richard. It has shown me how to defend myself which is what I needed when someone attacks me. I can still feel his eyes staring at me and there is his laugh, it is so loud you couldn't mistake it from anyone's. I really hate him, after what he has done to me. I could just imagine what I could do to him, now I do Taek-won-do it has given me enough courage to confront him if I had the opportunity to, but that will never happen, thank god.

My Nan Hoy and Uncle Frank came down to visit me for the weekend, which I thought was nice of them. While they were down David and my Uncle Frank popped into Asda, while my Nan and I sat in the car. I decided to go to the toilet, so I left me Nan in the car and walked in the store. As I came out I went to go around a customer that was at the trolleys. The trolleys were stacked out three a breast, so I went to go around the back of the customer not looking at the right of us. I never noticed a large pillar, of course I did not; I am partially sighted in my right eye so of course I didn't see it. Anyway I walked straight into it. Of course it knocked me out stone cold and cut above my right eye, and gave me a massive black eye.

My Nan rushed over to me, like any grandmother would. She was worried sick. But later in the hospital I assured her that I was alright, even though I had a great big black eye. I asked my Nan not to tell my mum, I would tell her in my own time. I stayed in hospital overnight but was allowed to go home the following day. Whilst I was in hospital they were not sure whether to let me see myself in a mirror or not because of my black eye might cause me to have a fit or not, but I was alright.

A couple of days later I went to Taek-won-do, not to take part just to watch. As I walked in everyone looked at me as if I had been in a fight or something. I had to assure them that I hadn't been in a fight, whereas I had just walked into a post at Asda. I was off from Taek-won-do for three weeks with this eye, but don't worry when I get back I was as strong as ever.

2001

It was time to get a new car. The next car we got was a green Zafra, which was an X registration plate number. This car was comfortable to sit in and had plenty of room to put things in the boot.

This year we went on holiday with Diane and Brian; we went to the Isle of Weight. When we left, we went in Brian's car but something started to go wrong with the car, so we had to come back and change over to our car. So we ended up leaving Portsmouth in our car on a ferry heading for the Isle of Weight. It was the first time David and I had ever been to the Isle of Weight. A couple of months before Brian had said to me, all seriously like, don't forget your passport? A couple of minutes later I realised he was joking, what a Wally, he must think I am too thick to think that you need a passport to go to the Isle of Weight.

When we got there it was a field with about 50 caravans in it. We found our caravan; it was in a line with the main house where there was a bar, which had a darts board and a pool table in it as well. The bar was not that much good because every night we had to drink something different because they ran out of whatever you drank that particular night. For instance, one night we would be drinking larger and the next night that would have run out so we would have to drink something else, and then the same thing would happen again. We got feed up so we got our own drinks in and drank them back at the caravan.

For entertainment, we visited the Needles, they were nice to see. We went down and saw them through the window in the side of the cliff face. One thing we loved to do is to play crazy golf. We stopped at many places to play this game. I can remember one game that we stopped at and it was this game of shot'n'put. It was a game of one to nine so you had to play it twice to play one to eighteen. The first round went fine; I didn't want to play again so I sat with the bags and watched the others play the final round. When it happened, David hit his ball and it began to roll and roll and roll towards the river. There was a 50 pence fine for each ball that goes in to the river. Now the ball rolled towards to river and David ran after it, his arms waving in the air and his legs from side to side. If only I had a camera. As he was running all three of us were laughing so much, it was hurting our sides. Luckily David did catch the ball, but it was so funny.

One night when we did go to the bar, David was drinking Pernod, blackcurrant and lemonade. He finished the bottle off; mind you there was about half a bottle in there anyway. When we got back to the caravan we started to play UNO (a game of cards); when Brian started talking about Harold and the battle of Nastings (Hasting), well that started David off he started talking about Arnold. Brian thought David was joking but David was totally drunk; meanwhile Diane and I were laughing so much that we had pains in our sides.

The next morning David woke up, he could not quite remember exactly what had happened last night. Diane, Brian and I all said about Arnold and Harold and the battle of Nastings (Hastings), and he sort of remembered what had happened.

We only spent a week on the Isle of Weight. A couple of days near the end of our holiday I caught a really bad cold, it was so bad

David had to pop in to the nearest chemist on the island and buy some medication and tissues for me. So apart from me catching a bad cold we all enjoyed the holiday a lot, even the trip back to the main land.

2002

This year David surprised me by taking my up to London to have my photographs taken by a professional and to have my make-up done by an artist. We drove the car up to St Thomas' Hospital in London; then get a taxi from there to the place where they were taking the photographs because David had no idea where the place was and there was nowhere to park around there.

After the photographs were taken we were taken into a room and shown the photographs on slides. We had to choose seven slides out of thirty, but I think we made a good decision. They cost a lot of money, but as David said I am worth it seeing as it was a once in a life time opportunity and we should take it.

After we had been there we headed back home. On the way home we decided to pop in to see Ian Morrison to see how I got on in the grade-in that I took a few days before. It was for my green belt (my third grade-in for Taek-won-do). Ian said that I had failed; I knew that before he even said a word. He said I could have done my kicks a lot more firm; as for my punches they could have been a lot stronger so you could have said I was totally crap. So I have got to be a lot more firm and stronger in all my body movements. So next week I have got to be a lot stronger than before; and do you know what I was.

In a few months I retook my Taek-won-do third belt again and guess what, I passed it. I was so over the moon to have passed because I put so much in to it a Wally could have passed it. That must make a Wally. So that means I am a green belt, the next belt I am going for is my green belt blue tab, that is a hard belt but who knows I might get it.

This year we went on holiday with Diane and Brian to Great Yarmouth. David and I have been there before and enjoyed it so much that we wanted to bring Diane and Brian there too. We hired a chalet while we were there, which was one week.

While we were in Great Yarmouth we went on two of the trips. First of all we visited a place like 'Yesterday World'; it had a cinema with the old organ the played the music with the film shown. I thought it was fascinating because I had never seen anything like this before.

The second place we visited was a Water Garden'; this was next to a river but was a lake that had pathways up and down, in and out of it, so that you could walk all around it. At the end of it you came to the river, where sat a boat which you could pay to go on to go around the river, which gave a tour on the river life. It was quite interesting.

It was about lunch time when Brian and I were sitting in the chalet, David was in the kitchen and Diane was in the other room; when on the television came a clip about an airplane crashing into a sky scraper and then another one did the same. Brian and I thought that this was a clip for a film that was going to come on during the following week. We both stopped what we were doing then a few seconds later realised that this was no film but actually happening. Calling to Diane and David to come to watch this; they couldn't believe their eyes. Neither could we.

We only stayed in Great Yarmouth for one week, and during that week we used to pop over to the main club building for the bingo in the evenings. Then we used to go back to the chalet to play 'UNO' (the card game), Brian used to jokingly moan because he used to end up with all the pickups, it is just the way it worked out. That is what we always say.

2003

It was time to change our car, this time we are getting a Citroen Berlingo. We liked this car because it was comfortable and it was slightly higher off the ground than the other cars we have had before. There was plenty of room inside; it has a shelf above the front window screen and it also had boxes in its flooring in its back flooring to store thing in. Which means you could hide things in the floor without anyone knowing it was there.

We went on holiday for the third time with Diane and Brian to a place near Portsmouth. We found our chalet alright, but we were not satisfied with all the workmen and dust going on all around us. We had to keep the windows closed all the time to keep the dust out, and one day we could not use the toilet or any taps because they were turning the water off.

Just down the road from the chalet was a butterfly site that also had a crazy golf on site. We looked around the butterflies, they were beautiful. After we had a drink, then it was time for the golf. It was a bit crazy but it was a laugh.

Another trip we went on was in Portsmouth around the harbour. We would have gone around the docks and around the Mary Rose (the famous boat), but it would have cost us over £76 for the four of us. That was for one disabled, one old age pensioner and two adults. It is so pricey, so we went to see how much the small boat was charging and guess what; they cost a fraction of what it cost around the docks. So we chose those instead.

The small boat showed us more boats/ships than we would have seen if we had gone around the docks. The boats/ships we saw were the big war ships; it was good to see them and to see how big they really are. When we were half way round we stopped at the 'Submarine Museum', where we got off and looked around there. It was an interesting museum. Part of it was to go inside a real submarine; even I had to duck my head to go through parts of the submarine, but we all really enjoyed ourselves a great deal and I learnt a lot about submarines that I did not know before.

This was the second time David had shingles. He had it on his left leg; it was horrible to look at. He had it before so he knew what to do. Luckily I have never caught it, and I would never like to catch it. Apparently it's like a rash with a burning sensation and it is very painful. According to the doctor you cannot get shingles more than once, I don't think much of this doctor because this is the second time David has caught it.

2004

It was in January when Diane and Brian asked us if we would be prepared to look after their foster son, Stephen in the summer while they go on holiday abroad; we said yes we would love to. As Stephen was their foster son we would have to fill in some forms for a police check and so forth. We did this in January to give them at least five months to check our records out.

Diane and Brian thought that our papers had been all checked out, so had we, seeing as we hadn't heard anything from social services. The week before they were due to go Diane telephoned the social services up to make sure it was alright. Social services said that our records have not gone through, so Stephen could not go to us, instead he was to go to this children's home. Diane and Brian were furious with social services but what could they do?

The day before they were due to go, they telephoned up the children's home to make sure Stephen was going there. To their surprise the children's home said 'No Stephen cannot come here because the home is full up of refuge children'; so Stephen will have to go somewhere else. The only other place for him to go is with us, so that is where he went.

Stephen must have been with us for about five days, when Stephen's social worker turned up out of the blue. She said that she was not happy with Stephen being with us and that she was looking for another place for him to go to. Stephen said that if she moved him

he would run away from that new home. So she had no option but
to leave him where he was. She said that she would pick him up
Friday, just to take him out for a chat; she will be there at 4.30pm.

On Friday, we waited until 4.30pm and there was no sign of her.
She eventually turned up at 5.20pm and David had a go at her, all
she said was 'Well I am here aren't I?' I mean that is no way to speak
to anyone, especially in front of a foster child. When they came
back she dropped Stephen off and that was the last we saw of her.
We told Diane and Brian about all this when they got back from
their holiday and they were not very impressed.

It was a warm sunny day in the month of June. It was David's
birthday (6th June), his brother had invited us both over to his place
for a bar-be-q; we said yes.

We arrived over there; it was running mad with children, mainly
his brother's grandchildren and a few of his own children that had
already grown up. The only soba one there apart from the children
was his common-law wife and that was because she did not drink.

David's brother was like his usual self, drunk and full of dope. I
feel sorry for the little kids because they are shown one side of
the fence and not the other, so they don't know what is right or
wrong. Anyway at least there is one person in the house hold that
has common sense to keep them of the booze and that is the
common-law wife.

We did not stay there for too long as we know when to leave and
that is when David's brother has had a little too much. So we make
up some excuse to get away and make our exit short and sweet.

2005

David had gone round by the old school house in New Romney, Kent, when he noticed that there was a computer class going on inside. So he went inside there and inquired about it, not for himself but for me. He did all this behind my back. So without my knowing I was now a member of this computer class.

When I started I found it quite easy because I had done most of the work before when I had been at South Kent College in Folkestone, Kent; the only thing that I found hard to do was the 'database', but that was not to come until the OCR Level 2 Certificate for IT Users (New CLAIT).

It was silly who would use half of the things you would do for level 1, I mean I know you would use at least two of the things you would do for level 1. The things that are mainly used for level 1 are: Using a computer and Word processing, the things that are not mainly used are Spread sheets, Graphs & charts and Presentation graphic. Those three things don't appear as an everyday thing. I mean I wouldn't use them would you?

Now it is the same with level 2, there is only one thing there that really comes to an everyday use; and that is Create, manage and integrate files. The other three don't come into use. They are: Spread sheets, Databases, Graphs and charts. I completed these two exams in the first six months. Meanwhile there were some workers there and it took them six months to do just the word processing part, and that was the easiest part of it.

My Nan Hoy had been ill for some time; she had been in hospital for quite a while. I was around Ian's when my mum telephoned me on my mobile that my Nan had died. Trust my Nan to choose this day of all days to die on, the same day as the Pope. The Pope died this morning whilst my Nan died this afternoon.

The funeral was interesting, but overall a bit sad. Two of my cousins were there and they and they told me that my Uncle Frank had sexually assaulted them both and they asked me if he had ever touched me in any way, I couldn't lie; he had touched me but that was a long time ago, when I was about 6/7 years old. They wanted me to go to social services with this information against Uncle Frank. I didn't really want to but until one of them told me off the cases he had touched her I felt it my duty, but my case seemed so petty compared to theirs.

I did all I said I was going to do and told the social services. The next thing I knew was that my mum was on the telephone to me saying I was a liar and that Uncle Frank had never been over on such a day. How was she supposed to remember way back then, when I was six/seven; after all I can only remember a few things; and it is things like this that stick in people's minds. And it was because of my mum saying that that squashed the case, so my Uncle Frank was let of the case. In a way I was relieved because I really do like my Uncle Frank. I must write a letter to him to apologise to him for the hurt I have coursed him, but I don't know where to start.

It was in June when David had just been round Diane's the day before about making her a flower box and what flowers she would like in there.

He had just finished making it and was just taking it over to her house across the road. They were out at that particular moment, so David left it round the back in the garden. David heard them pull up in their car, so he went over to tell Diane about the flower box.

About an hour had past when we heard a siren, we thought nothing of it; that was until Aimi (Diane's youngest daughter) knocked at the door. She came in, her face was full of tears, she said her mum's dead. We just couldn't believe it, Diane dead. Aimi said that she was asleep when she gave a sudden gasp of air and that was it. Emma (Aimi's sister) gave her mouth to mouth until the ambulance got there, but it was no good she was gone.

Diane's funeral was lovely the amount of flowers was lovely. She had a horse and carriage. The carriage was glass so you could see the coffin inside; it looked so beautiful, all nice and white, smothered in flowers from her daughters and her foster son, let alone her husband Brian.

I am still doing my Taek-won-do, and this time I have passed yet another belt. So this time I am now on my fourth grade-in which means that I am now green belt blue tab. The next grade-in, blue belt; seems so hard but I will try but it is harder than the last four. I don't think I will be able to get my blue belt but I will give it a go.

In this year things began to get on top of both of us. Nobody would listen to either of us, it did not matter where either of us went people just turned their back and went in the opposite direction, even the doctors. We had even talked about committing suicide, and we were getting very close to doing it.

This one particular Friday, David and I went to collect my repeat prescription from the chemist and it was not there. So David went round the doctors to see where it was, it had not been written. The receptionist then suggested that we make an appointment to see the doctor that evening, he agreed.

During that day we both were getting all our medication together for our suicide pack. We put our medication into the Camper and drove off; we got as far as Tenterden, Kent. When we got there David got his mobile out and telephoned the police up and started to talk to a police officer. The police officer talked to David who was talked out of the suicide which he was slowly coming out of. But me, well I was getting angrier and angrier as each minute went past. David put the police officer on the mobile to me and I just gave him a lot of negative chat back, and gave the mobile back to David, and then got up and went into the back of the Camper and got hold of all the medication and went to prepare it all for taking. David had agreed over the mobile to meet the police officer at our local doctors' surgery, all he had to do was get me to agree to go there with him too.

David finally got me to agree to go to the surgery with him. When we got to the surgery there was no sign of anyone else so we went straight in to see the doctor, there wasn't even any sign of the police either. We talked to our doctor about my prescription and what was the matter with the both of us, he actually listened to the both of us. After that we went out of the doctors' room where we were met by two police men. One of the police officers said something to David; I am not sure what they said, but one of them arrested us. I could not believe my ears when they read our rights out to us. They lead us out of the surgery, and towards the police car. David asked if he could take his car, they said no, he could leave it in the surgery car park. So he did. They drove us up to the mental health unit in the William Harvey Hospital, Ashford, Kent.

There we were shown to a waiting room, where the police officers told us to wait for someone to come. About 10-15 minutes later this man and woman came both holding sheets of paper. They mainly talked to David who did most of the talking. The man said that he wanted to keep David in and send me home, I said that was not a very good idea, he took me out of David's ear shot and asked me why I said it was not a very good idea. I said because I knew where all the medication was and I knew what to take. The man said that in this case I think we had better keep you in as well. Instead of keeping me at the Mental Health Centre with David they were going to send me to the one in Margate, Kent. That was only for one night, and then they brought me back to the Mental Health Centre here in Ashford, Kent.

When I got to the mental health centre in Margate I was taken upstairs to where was about a dozen other men and women, some were shouting at each other about something or other. I sat down in an armchair, not saying a word to anyone. Nobody spoke to me, so I didn't speak to them. When it came to evening meal, everyone else went and got something to eat, while I stayed seated and did not eat anything. It was about mid-night before I was shown where I was to sleep.

I hardly had any sleep that night; I spent most of the night standing up looking out of the window. I did try to sleep a little but I could not sleep on that bed, so I tried to sit on the floor. I found that more comfortable. Mind you even though I found that more comfortable I still couldn't sleep.

Throughout the night the staff kept an eye on me because I threated to kill myself the day before and for all they knew I could still do it if I had the right drugs or equipment with me; but of course I did not but that did not stop them from looking.

All the next day I spent it in the room that was originally an interview room but was changed into my bedroom the night before. The only time I was free from being watched was when I went to the toilet. When it came to breakfast and lunch, I passed on them both. I just was not hungry. That meant that I had not had anything to eat since yesterday breakfast.

Later that afternoon I was sitting on the bed when I suddenly fell to the floor with a fit, it only lasted a few minutes but they did not know that I suffered with epilepsy, but they did after this one. I came round in my own time, but I was a little dazed as I was sitting on the bed. The gentleman who was watching me asked me if I wanted anything to eat, I said no thank you. He said how about a little rice; it took a little while for me to agree to a little rice. When he brought me the rice, the first lot I couldn't eat because it had sweet and sour sauce on top of it, and I don't like that. So he went and got me some more. I only had about a third of it and then I was full up, I think he was disappointed about the amount I ate or didn't eat.

I was only to stay at this centre for one night as they found a bed for me at the mental health centre in Ashford, which was good for me because I will be close to David. I arrived at Ashford centre when it was very dark, so dark that it was all lit up.

When I got inside the centre I was still under watch. It did not matter if I went to the toilet or not, a female staff went in there with me, but otherwise they took turns to sit with me.

On the first night at Ashford I can remember going to bed and a male member of staff sitting in a chair at the door to watch me. The next thing I think happened was I had an epileptic fit, and the male staff did not know what to do because he did not know I was epileptic, so he called my husband David up from the floor below.

The next thing I remember was waking up in a hospital bed in a new room in one of their new wards. It came to dinner time and like I had done before I refused to eat anything. I did this for the next three/four days, so the nursing staff were getting a bit worried because I was refusing to drink as well. So what they did was put a drip into me, the trouble was finding a vein. You see it is almost impossible to find a vein to put or take blood out of me. I stayed in this part of the hospital for about five days; then I was taken back up to the centre up stairs.

I was under watch for two/three weeks, it was a bit annoying especially when you want to go to the toilet especially when you want to go for number two's. It was embarrassing when you can't help it but you do a smelly one, that's when you have held it in for a few days but you can't hold it in for much longer.

I was relieved when I was let of watch and could go where ever I wanted without being watched or asked every step I made. This meant I could do some of the activities that some of the other patients/clients did. Some of the activities included pottery, computer work, a morning walk etc. I did all of these activities plus some others.

When I had to see the panel of doctors and social workers, they all suggested that if I stayed in for a further fortnight and if I had anything to say to talk to this particular social worker, and they pointed to this female social worker.

This fortnight went passed so quickly and whenever I wanted to talk to this social worker she was either off work or on night shift, so I gave up. Meanwhile I had written all my feelings down on paper, it seemed easier than saying it, plus I could remember more if I could write it down. One person I won't let read it is David, I do not know why but I will not let him read it at the moment, so I have given it to Brian and Emma, as they were the only people who I could call friends at that time.

After Brian and Emma's visit I felt a lot better, in fact I felt as though I didn't belong in a place like this anymore. The trouble was what or who do I tell that I don't belong here anymore.

David's nephew in Manchester was having a surprise dinner party and we were invited, the trouble was I was stuck in here. I saw the panel and they would not let me out for the weekend for some reason or other. Yet I was still determined to go out this weekend. About two hours before I was due to leave a young doctor (one of their specialists) came up to talk me out of going out this weekend; but I was having none of this I was going and that was that. I was going and that was final!!!

I left there on the Friday and was told to come back on Monday morning to see the panel of doctors and social workers to see what they have to say about me going out without their permission.

We arrived at David's sister's Sue later on Friday night. When we got there we stayed up for a cup of tea and a quick chat, then we went to bed.

On the Saturday evening we drove our car to the Chinese restaurant, then our nephew wouldn't recognize our car so he wouldn't have any idea that this mum and dad would be in the restaurant. He was surprised when he came in the restaurant because he thought it was just his family not everybody else like David and me. It was a nice meal. The only thing that spoiled the evening was his two children putting soap over the handles of the toilet doors so that anybody using the toilet could not grip hold of the handle properly. But children will have their fun. Apart from that it was a nice evening.

On the Sunday before we went home Sue cooked us dinner, which was very nice of her seeing as this was Mother's Day. She also cut my hair for me, it needed cutting badly. After she had finished we said bye to everyone then got into our car and headed for home.

On the Monday we left to go to the centre at the William Harvey Hospital, Ashford, Kent. We waited in the centre for three hours before we were seen; there was a lady who was let out a week ago before me. She was seen before me and it was all thumbs up for her.

At last it was my turn to see the panel. I walked in with confidence, which showed the panel that I did not belong in a place like this. I told the panel of my plans to get better and that my husband was going to help me and that I was going to help my husband get better by encouraging him. So all the panel could do was let me go, so that is what they did.

Once I came out of the centre I felt a lot better, I felt as though I was like a bird that had just been let free.

I had been given a fortnights worth of tablets by the centre but I had to get my repeat prescription re-done by the local doctor. So I went to see my local doctor as soon as possible. He changed one tablet but apart from that he did not do anything to the list, so he just did the repeat prescription as the doctor at the centre did it.

I had gone back to playing darts but it was not the same without Diane being there. It just felt empty. I am seriously thinking about leaving and joining another darts team, that's if this other team will have me.

We decided to spend this Christmas and New Year away in Dubai. It was alright over there. It was very hot during the day and a bit sticky during the night. While we were over there we met up with one of David's internet buddies and his family. We met up with him and his family twice out of the two weeks we were over there. They wouldn't let us pay for anything even though we had plenty of money and they were hard up.

Our day began with us sun bathing, we did this until 1pm then we went to the massive shopping centre. I would say it was bigger than Lakeside, Essex. In this shopping centre there is one section just for jewellery, this has no price marked on it because you went in and you bartered for it. David got me a lovely necklace, and he only paid a fraction of the price it is worth. Then we would come back to the hotel because there was a choice of restaurant on each floor, so one night you could have Indian and the next you could have Mexican etc. There was also a cinema connected to the hotel.

2006

In this year my worst dreams came true; you know that dream that you stand at the head of a coffin and you look at the person inside of the coffin and you hate to think of the person; yes it is your mum. Your sweet mum, well in my case not so sweet, my mum she was so big you couldn't even carry her out in the coffin when they announced her dead, they had to push her out on a trolley.

The funeral was sad, I must admit I did cry; although I said I wouldn't but I did. It was held at St Paul's Church, Addlestone the same church I was christened and married in. The only difference with the church now is that it has had its insides all taken out and chairs instead of benches put inside.

I was surprised at the number of people that turned up for my mum's funeral. There was Molly from the newspaper shop. There was my friend Sandra with one of her five sisters and their mum, Maureen. After the church service, we had to go to Mortlake Crematorium to cremate her because this was the nearest place that has the largest coffins to take a large coffin like my mum.

I was having problems with my periods; I kept on bleeding none stop. First of all I had to go to the doctors then I had an appointment up at the hospital. At the hospital, I had to see a doctor and he said that there are several ways around stopping the bleeding. There was the coil, something else and the hysterectomy. He asked which one I would prefer I said that we had been talking about this and we had decided that the best choice would be the hysterectomy. The doctor said that was fine and that the nearest would be in about 4-6 weeks, I said that would be fine.

About four weeks' time I went up to the hospital for a pre-op, which is where they fill in all the forms ready for when you go in. my forms were easy to fill in; the only thing they had to make sure is when I go under for the operation they use the right one; because if they use the wrong one I could out fitting with epileptic fits, which is not a good thing because I end up in intensive care for a few days.

Today is the day I have my hysterectomy; I have to be in the hospital for 9pm. A funny time I know, but it was the time on the letter; my operation is about 11pm. Before the operation they said that it would be painful, so there would be morphine there when and where I need it.

I had the operation, it was no way near as painful as I expected it to be. The only bit of pain I got was when I started to move to go to the toilet after I was disconnected from the tube that connected you to the toilet tube. It took me several times to go to the toilet each hour, so I had to go 3-4 times each hour. I was alright going for number ones' but I found it a struggle doing number twos'. But by the second day out of four I finally did it, and what a relieve it was.

I was in there for four days, and they let me go. They said to go back in a week's time to have the pins out; I did not realise how big the pins were. But in a week's time I went back to have them taken out. I lost count after twelve.

Right now is the time that I could do with talking to my mum, but I can't can I because she is not with us anymore, because the silly woman is dead. Why did she have to die when she did? Just when I needed her, oh well, life must go on.

In this year I got terrible pains in my chest and down my left arm. I went to my local hospital, the William Harvey in Ashford, Kent; but they did nothing. So as we were driving up towards London anyway we decided to pop in to St Thomas'. As it was I was having an epileptic fit when I was due to go in.

I was in there for about a fortnight, whilst I was in there I had a number of tests done on me. I know one thing that was not related to any of the problems of the pains in my chest and the epilepsy was on my left hand my fingers kept on going white, it was just the tips of them.

The test was done on the last day of my stay in there. They also did a scan of my heart; that was alright. The scan of my left wrist showed that there was the main vein that was going along and then it suddenly went all narrow for a short time, then it went back to normal. Now because of the narrow part of my vein my blood cannot flow properly, which causes the tips of my fingers to go white and numb. I asked the doctor if there was a cure for this and he said there is an operation that could fix it or otherwise you could just learn to life with it, but to have the operation it costs money because you have to go private.

We decided to spend Christmas and New Year away this year, so we decided to go to Egypt. It was warm during the day but very cold at night. It was a lovely place to visit, but the people/beggars were always under your nose; you had to always push them away, apart from that it was lovely. The cost was reasonable too, some things you wanted to look at when you wanted to go somewhere were quite cheap, but when the beggars were pushing their wear up your nose were quite expensive.

We met one of the workers' of the staff that worked in the little shops on the hotel. His name was Michael; he had two workers with him as well. He sold rugs, table clothes and many other things. While I was there I brought a shawl, it was really nice. It came in useful because one of the trips we went on the women had to cover their head with a shawl or something and that is where the shawl came in useful.

We spent Christmas and New Year out there. The hotel that we stayed in put on a show to celebrate both the New Year and Christmas celebration; we thought both shows were very good. Mind you we did not stay to see all of the New Year celebration show because we had to be up early next morning to catch our coach to the airport.

2007

It is time that we have to change our car. We have decided to get a red Renault Kangoo, I can only remember the first four letters/numbers of the registration plate, and they are GL55. We chose this car because it was the same height as the Berlingo. Another reason why we chose this car was because it was ready and waiting on the forecourt for us to take away. It is a red car and I hate red cars but in this case I will make an exception.

Well my darts team, the British Legion have finally finished, so I finally plucked up enough courage to ask the Bailiff Sargent, St Mary's Bay if I could join them; and they said yes.

So on the Tuesday I went down to the Bailiff Sargent and they introduced me to the landlord and his wife, who fitted me out with one of their t-shirts, which fitted nicely.

I think I surprised my new team because of my drinking habits. You see, every time they saw me drinking at the British Legion I used to drink coke or soft drinks, but when I ordered my drink I ordered sherry. Now that did surprise them, so now I am known as the sherry drinker. It doesn't both us.

It was like Halloween we were playing darts away at the Ship pub in Dymchurch, Kent. When I was drinking my usual drink, sherry and the rest of them were drinking the green drink, whatever it was they were drinking it threw straws. So Helen (one of the members of the team) suggested that I should drink my sherry threw a straw, like a Wally I agreed to. I only drank one glass of sherry threw a straw though, because it made me go all tipsy.

By the time the evening was up I was well and truly drunk. Mind you I did win a tube of pringles (potato crisps). I got out of Helen's car alright with the help of Jackie (another member of the team). Jackie walked me to the door; that was fine. Now I managed to get the front door key out of my bag fine, it was getting my key into the door that was the problem, but lucky for me Jackie was there to help with that. That was after I dropped the pringles four or five time on the floor before Jackie took the key off me.

The next morning I opened the packet of pringles, the top half were alright; it was when I got down to the bottom half I wondered what had happened to them. Then it all came back to me, last night and the pringles and the key, I remember. I am never drinking threw a straw again.

The following Tuesday Jackie had told Helen about the key and the pringles, and they are never going to let me live that down. But that is alright, I have a thick skin so I can take it. After all I married David and he is always joking about with me. He has taught me to take jokes about myself because if I can't take jokes about myself then I can't take jokes about life. This is true.

We decided to spend Christmas and New Year away, so we decided to spend it abroad in Tunisia. The cleaning staffs were ever so nice and friendly, and that makes a difference when it comes to running a hotel. The entertainment crew were excellent for what they were. They were so funny, when they were supposed to be and serious when they were supposed to be. Now that's what I call entertainment.

Now the cleaning staff, the lady that did our room was ever so nice, she washed our floor every morning, changed our bed every day. In fact she did everything you would expect a normal cleaner to do but it is the way she did it that made it special.

2008

This year was a sad year because although Chris (David's sister) had been diagnosed with cancer before she had got rid of it before too, but this time she had been diagnosed with it again but this time it was all over her body. So she had so many months to live.

With the treatment that Chris was having it was making Chris lose all her hair, the poor thing, I feel so sorry for her; I would hate to have to go through that. As Chris knew that she was going to die she planned her funeral, she even planned her coffin and what hymns wanted sung and what music she wanted played. She had it all planned, Phil her ex-husband was going to pay for it because he still felt something for her even though they were divorced.

Chris's final week was a sad week. She was in hospital but wanted to spend her final week at home, so she was brought home. Her daughters: Nicki, Lisa and Aimee, and her granddaughter Jodie, all nursed her as well as looked after their own families. David and I visited every day.

The day came for Chris's funeral. We picked Ron up from Lydd, Kent to go up to Harlow, Essex. We got stuck in a traffic jam on the way up there, but we arrived just in time, just as they were going to leave. Our niece Nicki had arranged with one off the family friends to take me as David was going in one of the black cars that Chris had set aside for her brothers and sister and Ron; she had also set two black cars one aside for her children and one for her grandchildren.

When it came to carrying her coffin in to the church, St Stephens Church, David, Peter, Phil and Denis did the honour of being four of the six people to do it. The church service was nice Chris had set it out nicely. After that we followed the coffin out of the church and went on up to the crematorium.

The service at the crematorium was short but peaceful. After we all went outside and waited until we all were gathered into a group. Once we were ready someone brought out a basket with white doves in it. It was for Nic, Lisa, Aimee and the grandchildren to let free for their mum/grandmother, which I thought was nice of Chris to have thought of.

This summer we decided to go to Tunisia after all there is nothing holding us back now. We have no ties to keep us down so we might just as well go for it. The temperature out there is in its 90's. So we better make sure that we take plenty of sun cream with us.

2009

It is time that we got a new car; the next car that we got is a grey/blue Mazda 5 GF58 YBW. The day after we picked the car up we headed for Gatwick, because we were due to fly off to Tunisia for a three week holiday in the sun. Sod the cold winter weather we prefer the nice warmth of the sunny weather of Tunisia.

This year we spent January and June/July out in Tunisia; we made some friends with some of the staff and some of the other guests. In the January holiday we got off the plane in Tunisia and the sky didn't look to promising. We went through the check-in desk and got our luggage and came out the other side and all of a sudden it was a thunder storm, the rain was coming down so hard, the thunder and lightning was so wild it was unbelievable, even our suitcases got wet. That shows how hard the rain was. By the time that we got to the hotel it was all sunny again but you could see some of the puddles where the rain had been.

When we came home it was in the middle of the night and guess what we had problems with our brand new car, it would not start. Luckily for us there was a warden going around in his van and he fixed our car. It was just where it was new the battery had not charged up enough to start, so the warden started our engine and told us to go and see our garage tomorrow. So with the car all up and starting we finally got on our way home. The time being 1.40am and we had an hour and a half drive ahead of us before we got home.

It was in December when we decided that we would pay some of that money back that we took of David's real dad Arthur, so we went up to see him in his flat in Folkestone, Kent. We went with £1000 in cash to give to Arthur. Arthur seemed pleased to receive the money. We took Arthur to lunch once a week that is before we were away on holiday. He seemed quite happy in all the different places that we took him, and afterwards we took him to the Bailiffs Sergeante, St Mary's Bay, Kent. Which is my local pub who I play darts for. Arthur knew one of the staff that worked there from way back, so he found someone to talk to.

2010

It is January and we are going on holiday to Tunisia for three weeks. It is lovely weather, like an English summer. We come out here twice a year because we love this place so much. We get on with all the staff and we treat them with manners and hopefully they will treat you the same back.

In January we met two people named Brian and Valarie, they were not married just good friends. Valarie lives down Devon way, whereas Brian lives up London town. Brian must be well off or something because he pays for himself and Valarie to have six weeks there in Tunisia. Valarie said that six weeks is a bit much for her, she said she would prefer a three week holiday instead.

David is such a sweet heart because you see I have got a thing for white gold and he has brought me a new wedding ring made of white gold. My original wedding ring which I wear on my right little finger, anyway where was I oh yes, David being such a sweet heart because he brought me a white gold necklace for my birthday, which we spent away in Tunisia. I was 38 years old, I can't wait until I am 40, I don't know why but I can't wait, I want to have a party at home but who knows what will happen.

How about this for my 38th birthday, I had a trip to the dentist in Tunisia. It was a nice friendly dentist, nice and clean. I had a filling and a tooth to be taken out. Also while I was there another filling came out but he never did anything for that tooth. But with the filling and tooth he took out he didn't charge too much, which I was surprised at because I thought dentists charged a lot.

When we came home Great Britain was in a stand still because it was snowing. It had been snowing and it had turned to ice, then it had snowed again on top of that. It even had snowed in St Mary's Bay, Kent. Which is a rear thing to do, but it had only lasted for a few days.

After we had been home a few days we went to the travel agents to book our next holiday to Tunisia. It seemed silly booking up for our summer holiday so soon after coming back from our winter holiday, but we had the money there to pay for it so why not pay for it. I mean we don't smoke or drink, so why not use the money to pay for a holiday? So that is what we are doing. The dates that we are going to be away are 16th June until 8th July early hours in the morning.

It was time for our summer holiday, and we are going to spend our 19th wedding anniversary out there. I am going to look forward to next year when we spend our 20th anniversary out here we will make it seem so special between the both of us, not that we don't anyway.

We made friends' with one of the staff called Ali-G; he is married with two boys, in fact his wife has just had his second son. He said to me he was not getting enough sleep because his baby boy was crying so much during the night. Ali-G wanted to stay friends so he gave me his address and mobile number, so I gave him mine. I will write to him as soon as I get home.

While we were there during the summer holidays David and I went into the Jacuzzi department where I had four types of massage performed on me per day for four days, whereas David had four types of massage, but had one each day. The reason why David only had one a day is because his blood pressure was high each day and the doctor at the centre said that he could not do most of the massage things, whereas I could do any of them I wished, so I had the choice of five different massages. I enjoyed them very, very, very much.

Back to earth, or should I say back to normal life. One thing that I enjoyed most about coming back to home is my bed; you can't beat your own bed. The comfort of the sheets and the mattress, it is sheer bliss.

One thing that we learnt while we were away on holiday was that our usual travel agents' was not going to be going to be our hotel Royal Kenz, Tunisia anymore, so that we would have to go there by another travel agents' that have now taken over the hotel. So the next day we went to Ashford, Kent to the nearest travel agents' to see about our next holiday in January 2011.

The way the travel agents' have organised our holiday is great because once we have got on the plane and got to Tunisia and got off in Tunisia, we get a taxi at the airport to the hotel, and at the end of our holiday we get picked up by a taxi and taken to the airport by a taxi. It seems great; there is no sign of any coaches, thank god because I get a bit wheezy on the trip by the coach.

We have organised our transport to and from the airport, we are going by taxi. Well it works out less by taxi than it does by parking at the airport, so we are saving some money by booking by taxi.

This holiday was cut short because of all the fighting that was going on in the countries around Tunisia and in Tunisia itself. We stayed six days out of the twenty-one days that we were supposed to have stayed there. Instead of getting the taxi back to the airport like we were supposed to we were all put on these coaches and taken to the airport. The first airport that we were supposed to go to we were stopped by fighting across the motorway so we were sent back to our hotel for about 3-4 hours, then we were taken to this new airport that was not supposed to open until the middle of the year (the time being December/January). At this new airport nobody knew where anybody was supposed to go so we stood in this queue for about eight hours not knowing if it was the right queue or not! Thankfully it was the right one, but we finally got on a plane and took off at about 1am.

We were pleased to get out of the fighting in Tunisia but we had another journey ahead of us, the plane we all had got on was not going to Gatwick which we all wanted but instead it was going to the Middle East, which was way off course and the people who organised this plane knew this so they arranged a coach for the passengers who are for Gatwick could get back to there, that included us. The coach that we had to take us back was useless; it did not have any heating so it meant that we had to freeze, and the emergency door was broken so it was always bleeping so it was almost impossible to get any sleep in the 5-6 hours journey to Gatwick.

Once we got to Gatwick we then went to the taxi rank to hire a taxi home because we knew that the taxi that we got up to Gatwick would be busy with taking the children to school (like they normally do), so we hired a taxi from the airport to take us home. We finally got home at about 8.15am, and we were totally shattered after all we have hardly had any sleep for 36 hours, maybe a bit more.

The next day we went to visit our local travel agents' about our holiday that was cut short about getting compensation, they said that we were defiantly due some compensation but they were not sure how much. They got David to fill in some forms and they sent them off, they told David and me to wait and they would let us know for the reply.

We waited, and when we got the reply we got just over £150, we both thought that was an insult, I mean we paid well over £1300 for that holiday, we didn't even spend a week out there and they didn't even give us a fifth. I think it is a disgrace.

A couple of weeks after our holiday we were walking out towards the car, when all of a sudden I had a black-out and fell down. I cut both my knees, the palm of my left hand, the top of my right hand and very badly bruised my right wrist. I thought I might have broken my right wrist, well I visited the Royal Victoria Hospital, Folkestone, Kent there walk-in centre and saw their head nurse. She was the one who said that it was broken (without an x-ray), so she put a plaster on it. It was a funny looking plaster; I have never seen a plaster looking like this before. She never put a stocking on it first but instead she just put the cotton wool on first, then on top of that the plaster of Paris but that was on only half of it the other half was just cotton wool. Then she let me go saying to me to come back in three weeks to take it off.

Well four days had gone by and I was getting suffer pain in my right wrist, so David decided to take me up to the William Harvey Hospital, Ashford to let them have a look at my wrist. The nurse that took the plaster off my wrist said that she had never seen a plaster like that before. For starters she said that there was no stocking on it, second, the way the nurse had put the cotton wool on was wrong, she had put most of it around the wrist so that it was weighing the plaster down on what was supposed to be protecting it. And third, the plaster, well that was wrong it was not even protecting anything so that was a waste of time having it on there anyway.

So this new nurse sent me for an x-ray; that came back fine. I hadn't broken any bones but I had badly bruised my wrist instead, so the nurse just put my arm in a sling and told me to take a couple of paracetamol if the pain gets to server, and with that she let me go. I was lucky it was not my left hand otherwise I would have been in the s**t (excuse my French) because only having the use of one hand you tend to relay on that more than ever. If someone came up to me and offered me the use of my right hand I would probably say to them 'no' because I have gone 22 years without the use of it and have managed fine without it.

It was in July when we heard of Arthur's (David's dad) fall in Folkestone, Kent. We heard about it when he had another fall in hospital and bashed his left check and eye on a table. The state of him it looked like Tyson had bashed him let alone a table. He was a bit unsure of his surroundings and of the people in it, especially me! For some reason or other he kept on having a go at me, it was rather upsetting for me but I didn't let it show.

David's dad, Arthur was let out of respite about the middle of October and David never missed a day, he visited him no matter what the weather was like rain, wind, snow whatever David was there. I go with him most days except Wednesdays because I go to computer club. Towards the end of his stay in respite he was getting used to me, the only trouble now was I was getting used to the fact that he was going to keep on telling me to shut up even though I have not said a word, so I just laughed it off because I know it was only a joke!

On the 23rd October I was rushed to hospital with epilepsy. Well it all started a couple of days before I got pains in the centre of my chest and down my left arm, so David called an ambulance. They came and did their business, took my blood pressure, etc. They gave me a little spray under the tongue and that eased it a bit. Then they took all details off David then they got me ready to put me into the ambulance. At the hospital they just took my heart readings, blood pressure etc. After being in there for about 3 hours they said I could go home. They didn't say what was wrong with me just to go home, that was it!!

So on the 24th October I was rushed to hospital with epilepsy, the first lot for four years and it is all due to the signs of the pains in the chest the day before. The same pains that I had four years ago previously. They only kept me in until Monday evening because I am not on any medication for epilepsy so there is nothing they can do for me, so they might as well send me home. The day that I came out of hospital, Monday, I was still having fits but that didn't matter, because I was still coming out of hospital.

The trouble with epilepsy it wears you out so much for a couple of days so that you cannot do anything you would normally do, like darts. So on the Tuesday after I came out of hospital I felt like s**t, I felt as though I couldn't do anything, so David texted Helen and told her what had happened and said I would not be able to go to darts, Helen texted back 'ok hope she gets better soon.

David has recently been talking to a disabled woman on the internet called Donna. She sounds really nice. She lives at home with her mum and her brother who is married to this woman but is living with her divorced husband. It sounds a bit fishy to me!!

This Christmas we decided to spend at home, so we had been invited to David's Aunt Jenny's and Uncle Roger's for dinner and tea. David got the invite from the computer through the email part. Jenny wanted to know what starter we wanted beforehand; so David said that we would be having pawn cocktail, for main meal veal and vegetables' and for pudding Christmas pudding with brandy sauce.

It was Christmas day morning, it might be 1 am in the morning but its' still Christmas morning, and we can open our presents. I said to Natalie that I would wait until Christmas day until I would open my presents, and I have. We got a clock, candle sticks and a flower stand of Natalie. David got shower gel and aftershave while I got a watch and necklace of his sister Sue and brother-in-law Denis. My Dad sent us both a gift voucher worth £20.

We left about 9.40am to pick David's Uncle Dennis up to take him with us to his Aunt Jenny and Uncle Roger's. We arrived there at 10.15am; I was already with my red and white Santa's hat. After we had all seated down and had a cup of coffee, Jenny went through the menu; we all had pawn cocktail. Then there was veal cooked with cranberries and something else, I didn't like that; the veal I liked it was the cranberries, so Jenny cooked mine in something else, something I liked. Then there was Christmas pudding; most people wanted minced pies and there were two of us that wanted Christmas pudding with custard. That was dinner. The crackers were different, instead of being toys, they were bells and at the end of the meal you could play a tune because each bell had a number 1 to 8 on it and there was a song sheet with the numbers on it, and you played your bell when your number came up. I thought that was quite good.

After dinner we sat down and played with the bells for a while. Then we opened each other's presents. We got £20 worth of music shop gift vouchers; that can only be spent in one type of shop; we didn't mind, we had to go into Folkestone town shopping centre anyway.

At about 7.30pm we sat down for tea, to tell the truth I was still full up from dinner, but I made an effort. For tea we had three types of cheese, salad, bread, pickled onions, plus other things. I only had bread and cheese, if I had anything else I would have had felt uncomfortable.

We left there about 9.45pm, after we said out goodbyes' to Jenny, Roger and Arthur. We said to Arthur that we would see him again on Friday (New Year's Eve). By the time we got home it was quarter past ten, time I was in bed.

It was New Year's Eve; we went round Arthur's, just for an hour. Arthur is just like his usual self always telling me to shut up in his usual way, I just tell him to shut up back in my joking fashion way; and we just laugh, then David starts, then we all giggle.

We telephoned Ron up early to wish him a happy new year as we would not be over to wish him a happy new year; instead we had an early night. Instead of visiting Ron we asked him over for dinner tomorrow; and he said yes.

2011

So Ron came over for dinner on New Year's Day. We had a three bird roast, it was lovely. It was the first time Ron had ever tried this before. It consists of turkey, chicken and duck; it was lovely and it only costs £9.99 from Aldi from Hythe, Kent. Ron said that he enjoyed his dinner a lot.

In the middle of January I got a text from my dad saying that my younger brother Kevin had become a father again, he had become a dad to a boy, again. It's not as if I am even interested, which I am not. It is the fourth child he has had, all boys. I had been a God-mother to his first one. I was one of six God-parents; he had three God-mothers and three God-fathers. I don't know why he had that many God-parents a bit of waste of time if you ask me.

For my birthday Donna sent me a Tesco's voucher worth £20 and a birthday card that was handmade. I brought some new tops with the vouchers that Donna sent me, they were really nice.

This Friday's David father's Arthur's 79th birthday, he said that he does not want to go out for a meal, like we planned, because he said he could not eat their size meals which I agree with because I can't eat too big a meal too, so we are getting him a bottle of vodka instead. Arthur enjoyed himself very much with the vodka.

The Mazda Company called all the cars in because there was something wrong with the car, there was something wrong with the power steering. I am glad they called the car in because who knows what might have happened if they have left it. It took them three hours to fix, but as they say 'better safe than sorry'.

My dad text me in March to thank me for his birthday card, he also told me that my Uncle Frank had been charged for drunken driving. This is his third time for this offence. He has to go to court on the 17th March 2011, I think he should be sentenced after all the times he has gone out driving drunk, they should lock him up and throw away the key.

I texted my dad on the 17th March to see if he knew how my Uncle Frank got on in court; he telephoned a short while later. He said that my Uncle Frank got bound over to keep the peace for a year and a £400 fine. My dad said that he corrected my dad when he said that it was his third offence when in fact it was his fourth. My dad and I couldn't believe it and he only got bound over to keep the peace for the year, it we had been the judge we would have sentenced him. Well at least he has got something; he has to find a new job because he has lost his licence which also means losing his job.

I also learnt a few months later that my Uncle Frank and his friend had moved down to the Devon area where no-one knew him and so he could make a new start for himself. I couldn't blame him really because everybody knew his face up here and at least no-body knows him down there.

2012

It was January 18th when I am 40 years old, and I am really looking forward to becoming 40 because of several things: one—I am glad to be alive because when I was 16 years old my heart stopped three time; two—I am glad to be happily married to my husband, David who is my life stone for now and always.

For my 40th birthday I had a birthday party, which was a bit of a disappointment not because of the music which was great no faults with that, but with the guests. You see David's dad, Arthur, Uncle Dennis, Aunt Jenny, Uncle Roger, Aunt Lois and Cousin Darren and other half all turned up. So did Natalie, Emma and Tiana came too. From the women's darts team only Jackie and her other half and one of her daughters came, we were very disappointed with the rest of the darts team because they all said that they would come but in the end they didn't bother, well two can play at that game. They will not come to my party then I will not go to their darts games. It was the same with David's darts team, he invited them to my party but only Neil the captain turned up. We both were a bit hurt because they all had said two day previous that they would be there but then nobody turned up. David felt like giving his darts a miss too but he didn't.

It was about March when we were having problems with David's dad, Arthur and where he was living. It was not really with his dad exactly it was with a couple of his neighbours who lived opposite him. They used to go outside to smoke a cigarette and Arthur used to take the micky out of them and they didn't like it so they put a complete in to David's Aunt Jenny who was Arthur's landlady. Of course Jenny took things a bit too far and gave Arthur one month's notice to find another place to live. Even I know that you cannot give someone a month's notice like that, you have to give them two verbal warnings and one written warning before you tell them to go. So he is safe for the time being but we are looking for somewhere anyway.

We got in touch with this woman who helped us fill in the forms, confidently, that is what we were told by herself but when David and myself went down to see Jenny and Roger she told us something we had told this woman in confidence. So much for confidentiality!!

David and I walked up and down Folkestone town centre going in and out all the estate agents asking if they had any ground floor flats going up for rent. Most of them said no, but if we left them our name and number they would contact us if one came free in the future. The ones that said that they had something when we went to have a look at it with Arthur all had steps to climb up or down.

We even went to the council to see if they could help. They were of some help; they said that Jenny had no rights to throw Arthur out in streets. In fact the council did come up with a place for Arthur to live, that was until they found out something that happened a long time ago, then they said sorry you cannot have this place and you will have to look for a place to live by yourself.

We thought all was lost with finding a place for Arthur to live that was until this place came up. It was a two minute walk from the town centre, which was wonderful for Arthur who goes down town every day. His new flat is big enough for one person, which suits Arthur down to the ground. As you go through the front door on the left is the bathroom, straight ahead of you is the bedroom, turn right and you walk in to the kitchen and carry on and you come in to the living room. And that is Arthur's new home, small but big enough for one person.

Jenny was pleased to get Arthur out of the flat above her because she wanted it for one of her sons' to buy it and live there with his girlfriend and their baby and her children. Jenny's son has just recently had their baby so I expect Jenny is going to be spending every spare moment looking after that baby.

Arthur is enjoying his new flat. David and I visit his dad's flat twice a week: on Monday and Friday. We do the cleaning while we are there. I do the dusting and hovering, while David cleans the kitchen and the bathroom. After we have done this we go down the town and meet up with Arthur. Once we have meet up with Arthur we go and have a cup of coffee/tea.

Back to David and his darts team, well I thought that I would join his darts team so I put my name alongside David's name ready for the winter league. But before the winter league started there was a couples' match to play which gave Brian & Maggie and David & me a chance to play in a game. Brian & Maggie got knocked out on their first game and David & I got knocked out on our second game. On our first game we knocked out the captain of the women's team that I used to play for (I was pleased I knocked her out).

When the winter league darts team started we all went to play for a new pub, 'The Swan'. The landowner of this pub was Emma. The captain of the darts team is still Neil, and the vice-captain is Brian. The rest of the team is as follows: Emma, Stefan, William (Billy), and Keith, Maggie, David and me. When we play at home I usually do the score sheet because I fill it all in properly unlike anybody else.

Emma is a very thin woman who is about 5 foot something, but her bark is harder than her bit. Stefan is the chef for 'The Swan', so he has to always play the last players' game as he is always cooking the food for us to have about three quarters of the way through. He is about 5 foot 7ish if not taller. He is a tall slim man. Billy is a young man who is slim for his age. Keith is a middle aged man that is much taller than me.

I do get to play darts some of the time, for instance in the winter league five people get to play five games each so there are twenty-five games played altogether. I played my five games and on this particular game I won four out of five games; yes I was shocked too. The following week I won two out of five games. The following week we had a bad week because we were one player short so we had to let five games go so we had to start the game of as 0-5. By the end of the evening the final score was 3-22, we were ashamed of ourselves but there was nothing we could do. Maggie scored two and I scored one, neither David nor Brian scored any.

It was on the 11th December when David invited his Aunt Lois and her boyfriend Tony over for dinner. They arrived at about 6pm on this cold winter's evening. We sat down for dinner to a shepherd's pie, broccoli, cauliflower and Brussels sprouts (I hate Brussels sprouts) and gravy. To follow for pudding we had melon and grape mixed with honey, which went down a treat.

After dinner we had a good chat. I washed up apart from the two glass dishes and the sauce pan that David used for the gravy. Whilst I washed up David entertained our two guests Lois and Tony. They enjoyed themselves a lot and both said that we will have to come to theirs' after Christmas and the New Year. We said how much we had enjoyed ourselves and agreed with them for the New Year. We gave them their Christmas present and card and Tony said that he will give me theirs' tomorrow at the computer club. And he did.

The next day at the computer club I had a happy time, with all the gentlemen always picking on me. I must have 'mug' or 'pick on me' written on my fore head, but if they didn't pick on me I would think there is something wrong with them or me, but I know it is only for fun.

Well this is my story and my life. I hope you enjoyed reading my book because I enjoyed telling my life story to you even though it had happy and sad bits in it.

From Joanna